THE
BIRTH OF A NATION
STORY

FOREWORD

The *Birth of a Nation* motion picture, produced in 1915 and directed by the talented David Wark Griffith, was the first twelve reel motion picture ever made.

This Civil War and Reconstruction period film with its stirring battle scenes and portrayal of the confused, tragic postwar years, has been viewed by more than 100,000,000 Americans. The picture has been acclaimed for its stirring, panoramic sweep, its artistry and the introduction of many new movie techniques.

Some persons and groups bemoan the continued exhibition of the picture due to the racial problems in the story, which is adapted from Thomas Dixon's novel, *The Clansman*. The co-authors of the *Birth of a Nation* story, especially Roy E. Aitken, who owns controlling interest in the *Birth of a Nation* film, have clung tenaciously to the facts in relating the dramatic events surrounding the producing of this American epic, and its exhibition over a period of almost fifty years.

The record reveals that many minority groups have persistently and vigorously boycotted the showing of this motion picture, claiming that it creates racial problems. Perhaps it is the misfortune of the Negro race that certain members of it are shown to disadvantage in the *Birth of a Nation* film. History has shown that the minority of the liberated Negroes who were involved politically in the turbulent Reconstruction period were usually spurred to action and dominated by unscrupulous white carpetbaggers.

The white man, the red man, the yellow man, and the brown man have no monopoly on cruelty, hate, greed, rape or any other human failing. This has often been demonstrated in newspaper and magazine articles, in plays, short stories and novels. When the factual or fictional spotlight turns upon the Negro, as it does in some measure in the *Birth of a Nation* movie, he has no choice but to bear the scrutiny and the ignominy of it. In company with his white, red, yellow and brown brothers, he can only hang his head in shame. From such universal shame, perhaps Man will identify and study his family racial problem and begin to try to solve it.

This is said to be the age of inquiry and scientific approach. We ask readers of this book to regard this reportorial account of the *Birth of a Nation* story as an account of the impact of a great motion picture upon three generations of Americans. If the *Birth of a Nation* movie has a little dust on its garments and mud on its feet, these have inevitably been gathered by following realistic characters who almost always have feet of clay.

That the *Birth of a Nation* evidences much historical accuracy, and also dramatic truth, is attested by the many requests that come annually from colleges, universities, museums, private art and film groups, and others, to show the picture. Recently, parts of this historic film were shown on the British Broadcasting system and on the National Broadcasting System.

In a lengthy opinion on the *Birth of a Nation* in 1915 the National Board of Censorship said, in part, "If the picture tends to aggravate serious social questions and should therefore be wholly forbidden, that is a matter for the action of those who act on similar tendencies when they are expressed in books, newspapers or on the stage. On what basis of reasoning should a film play be repressed whose subject matter has already been allowed the freest circulation both in a novel and in a play?"

The Authors.

ACKNOWLEDGMENTS

This book was made a reality with the help of scores of interested persons. We are very grateful to Lillian and Dorothy Gish, Anita Loos, Mae Marsh, Gloria Swanson, and Enid Markey, for the information they provided about the early days of the movies when they were under contract to the movie companies which my brother, the late Harry Aitken, and I financed.

Dr. T. K. Peters, John Hampton, T. H. Cochrane, Teddy Shull, Mrs. J. Carling, Nick Tronolone, and Tom Kennedy, associates of long ago, contributed valuable data which enabled us to include many of the episodes in this book concerning the promotion of our motion pictures.

Chas. James, Bob Edwards, Austin Baird, and W. S. Griswold aided us with their recollection of nickelodeons, and of legal and historical matters pertaining to Midwest distribution of Majestic, Reliance, Triangle and Epoch films. Clark Wilkinson, Baraboo, Wisconsin, movie hobbyist, opened his impressive movie files for our inspection. Valuable newspaper and magazine articles were made available for study by the Waukesha County (Wisconsin) Historical Society, the Wisconsin Historical Society, Madison, Wisconsin, University of Wisconsin Library, New York Public Library, and the Museum of Modern Arts, New York, as well as the new Hollywood Museum, Los Angeles.

Kent D. Eastin, Blackhawk Film Co., Davenport, Iowa, contributed important film history data; Wallace Walthall, brother of Henry Walthall, furnished anecdotes about **Birth of a Nation** theater promotions, and Jessie Walker, Glencoe, Illinois, granddaughter of J. R. Freuler, early partner in Aitken enterprises, provided previously unpublished material about Freuler-Aitken negotiations. To all these people, we extend our sincere appreciation.

THE

BIRTH OF A NATION

STORY

BY

ROY E. AITKEN

AS TOLD TO

AL P. NELSON

A DENLINGER BOOK

AN OFFER IS MADE

Harry Aitken, whose vision and faith helped to shape the movie industry.

My brother Harry and I were viewing television in our family home in Waukesha, Wisconsin, one warm spring evening in April 1954, when the telephone rang.

Harry answered as I turned down the television sound. "Hollywood calling," said the operator in a carefully measured tone. "I have a call for Harry Aitken. Is he there?"

"This is he," Harry said quietly, and waited.

An assured, confident voice boomed over the wires. "Hello, Mr. Aitken. Are you the Aitken who owns controlling interest in the *Birth of a Nation* movie?"

"I am." Harry was not overly excited. We often received phone calls from people connected with theaters, universities, museums, and film societies wanting to show this famous Civil War period movie. For such is the interest in this, the most controversial motion picture of all time, which we, Harry and I, initially financed in 1913-14 and have been distributing ever since. A picture which *Variety Magazine* reported two hundred movie critics voted the greatest motion picture produced during the first fifty years of the industry.

"I'm Phil Ryan," the Hollywood caller said. "I represent a group of bankers and movie executives who are interested in remaking the *Birth of a Nation* as an entirely new picture."

Harry was taken aback and did not answer for a moment. This was the kind of production offer we had been working and hoping for ever since sound had been put on the old silent movie, back in the 1930's.

"Hello—Hello—" came back Ryan. "Did you hear me, Aitken?"

"I heard you," Harry finally replied. "You wanted to know if we'd deal on our rights to the *Birth*. Yes, we would. But we'd want a sizable sum—perhaps three-quarters of a million dollars. It's a great picture. Still playing after forty years in this country and in Europe. No one knows which Civil War picture grossed more—the *Birth* or *Gone With the Wind*. They're both top-notchers."

"I know that," said Ryan, "but the *Birth*

4

would have to be remade carefully and at a great cost to become a big box office attraction again. When can we get together in Milwaukee to talk about a deal? My backers want action."

Harry and Ryan talked for several more minutes. They finally agreed for Harry and me to confer with Ryan two days later at the Plankinton Hotel in Milwaukee.

I saw that Harry's hands were trembling as he put the receiver back on the cradle, and I'll confess that my heart was pounding, too. Was this the big deal we had looked for through the lean income years since 1930? The *Birth's* lush earnings had lasted from 1915 through 1926—an estimated gross of $60,000,000 paid by more than 100,000,000 movie patrons anxious to see the popular picture that had revolutionized the making of movies. All this despite bitter censorship battles, vigorous minority groups' opposition, picketing, and even political interference.

Controversial? Yes, even today. No other motion picture has won more lavish praise, or been more bitterly condemned. And this is the exciting photoplay to which Harry and I have played nursemaid and guardian for almost fifty years. Harry died in 1956. Today I am the sole guardian of the great picture, which, despite its stepped-up film speed in the sound version, still creates tremendous excitement wherever it is exhibited.

Controversial, too, was the ownership of the picture when it was first produced in 1914. D. W. Griffith, although he was our director and his salary was paid by our Majestic Film Company, let it be known, intentionally or unintentionally, that he owned the picture.

He *did not,* and he later had to backtrack on his claim. The truth is that the *Birth of a Nation* should be credited to a triumvirate. Thomas Dixon, the author and a Baptist preacher, wrote the books, *The Leopard's Spots* and *The Clansman,* on which the photoplay was based. David Wark Griffith directed the picture masterfully. And my brother Harry and I raised the initial $59,000 to finance the picture and have always held controlling interest in Epoch Producing Corporation, the company which owns the copyright.

Griffith's name is plastered all over the prints of the film and was featured in newspaper and magazine advertisements. He is entitled to that glory, perhaps, because he reached artistic heights in that movie which brought the motion picture to maturity.

But Griffith, although he had many opportunities to do so, never gave Author Dixon much credit or recognition, nor did he credit Harry and me for our herculean efforts in obtaining the original financing to put the *Birth* into production.

Why he did not, we never knew. But Thomas Dixon smarted under the slight for many years and frequently told Harry and me so. We felt as Dixon did that the great Griffith could have been a bit more gracious to his associates—to put it mildly.

Besides writing the books on which the *Birth* was based, Thomas Dixon contributed a great deal to the promotion of the picture. As a student at Johns Hopkins, he had met Woodrow Wilson, who was eight years his

Hedda Hopper, in the days when she was an actress with the Aitken film companies.

Gloria Swanson, a great actress who got her start with the Aitkens.

senior. Dixon was passionately interested in drama and yearned to become an actor. Wilson wanted to become a noted historian. Despite the differences in their aspirations and eventual careers, the two became lifelong friends. In 1915, Dixon and Harry arranged a private preview of the *Birth* at the White House. President Wilson also invited the Supreme Court Justices and a few others to see the picture. When the long, stirring Civil War film came to an end, Wilson wiped his eyes. "It is," he said sadly, "like writing history with lightning. And my only regret is that it is all so terribly true."

Although there were not supposed to be any press notices of this private showing of the *Birth,* the news traveled the Washington grapevine and word quickly spread in movie circles that a great motion picture had made the President weep.

From the opposite point of view, thirty-five years later, Max Lerner in the *New York Post* of June 1, 1950, wrote concerning a showing of the *Birth:*

"If you want to see an elaborate excuse for racist hate, presented in the guise of a movie classic, you will find it in David Wark Griffith's *Birth of a Nation.*

"I saw it the other night for the first time. Once is more than enough. I could have lived out the rest of my days in perfect serenity and presented myself in due course before the Angel Gabriel with complete assurance that the gates would not be swung closed against me merely because I had failed to pay obeisance to a classic of racist passions, rape and lynch-law.

Dorothy Gish with Walter Long, who played the part of Gus, Negro renegade in **Birth of a Nation**.

Louise Fazenda was a popular Aitken star.

"Having seen it, I want to tell you about it so that you may save your time for something better, and spare yourselves the ordeal. . . .

"The picture has been called an epic. It is just that—an epic of the rise of the Ku Klux Klan, with a justification of its birth and violence. I suppose the movie historians are enamoured of its handling of big crowds, and its battle and mob scenes, in the grandiose tradition which Cecil De Mille has dubiously carried on. But even on this score it has little that has not been done far better since in many Grade B Westerns. . . ."

Prolific novelist Rupert Hughes wrote after seeing the *Birth* for the first time in 1915:

"Hardly anybody can be found today who is not glad that slavery was wrenched out of our national life, but it is not well to forget how and why it was defended, and by whom, and what it cost to tear it loose, or what suffering and bewilderment were left from the bleeding wounds.

"The North was not altogether blameless for the existence of slavery, nor was the South altogether blameworthy for it or its aftermath. The *Birth of a Nation* is a peculiarly human presentation of a vast racial tragedy.

"There has been some hostility to the picture because of an alleged injustice to the Negroes. I have not felt it; and I am one who cherishes a great affection and a profound admiration for the Negro. He is enveloped in

Taylor Holmes in **Taxi,** one of Triangle's short features.

Anita Loos, a script writer for the Aitkens for many years, wrote the book, **Gentlemen Prefer Blondes.**

one of the most cruel and insoluble riddles of history. His position is all the more difficult since those who most ardently endeavor to relieve him of his burdens are peculiarly apt to increase them. . . .

"It is hard to see how this drama could be composed without the struggle of evil against good. Furthermore, it is to the advantage of the Negro today to know how some of his ancestors misbehaved and why the prejudices in his path have grown here. Surely no friend of his is to be turned into an enemy by this film, and no enemy more deeply embittered.

"The *Birth of a Nation* is a chronicle of human passion. It is true to fact and thoroughly documented. It is in no sense an appeal to lynch-law. The suppression of the picture would be a dangerous precedent in American dramatic art.

"If authors are never to make use of plots which might offend certain sects, sections, professions, trades, races or political parties, then creative art is indeed in a sad plight. The suppression of such fictional pieces has always been one of the chief instruments of tyranny, and one of the chief dangers of equality."

That the picture is still highly controversial today, and that minority groups work to prevent it from being shown, is demonstrated by the following item from the March 30, 1959, issue of *Film Daily,* a trade magazine:

"Cincinnati—A decision by the University of Cincinnati to prohibit the showing of the 1915 classic, *The Birth of a Nation,* in its eight-week Silent Film Festival aroused such a storm of protests by would-be viewers and the local newspapers, that the college board of directors quickly reversed the decision of Dr. Frank R. Neuffer, dean of the Evening College. The film will be screened as soon as another print becomes available.

"Several hundred persons attending the film festival were surprised and very much annoyed when it was announced at the evening session that another film was being substituted, because a score or so of local residents had filed protests. Among those who were protesting was Kenneth Banks, executive secretary of the National Ass'n for the Advancement of Colored People, who said the film 'distorted some historical situations.'

"As the result of cancellation of the film, local newspapers printed first page stories pointing out the 'invasion of academic free-

Dorothy Gish, Lillian's sister, was a comedy actress and starred in many pictures for Majestic and Reliance Motion Picture Company.

dom.' In later editorials, the newspapers declared the decision to reschedule the film 'was more befitting a university.' "

I could go on for pages quoting pro and con statements that have been made about the *Birth of a Nation* during the many years it has been exhibited in the United States and other countries. One of the cities in which it was banned until recently is otherwise liberal Milwaukee, a city barely twenty-five miles from my Waukesha home. And yet many colleges, universities, film societies, historical, and other groups show the picture regularly. Not so long ago it was re-run in London to a large audience. Parts of the picture were also shown on BBC.

Perhaps the *Birth's* greatest popularity is in the South where Wallace Walthall, our Southern distributor, appears with the show, lecturing about it—and he loves his job. He is a brother of the late Henry Walthall, who played the part of the Southern Little Colonel. His Northern sweetheart, Elsie Stoneman, was protrayed by winsome Lillian Gish. Elsie's father, Austin Stoneman, represents Thaddeus Stevens, the congressional leader in Thomas Dixon's *Clansman* who directed the punishment campaign against the South in the Reconstruction Era.

Why has the *Birth of a Nation* been so popular with movie patrons of several generations?

I think the reason is that the exciting, colorful picture deals dramatically with human and historical problems in this nation's most publicized conflict—the Civil War. So does *Gone With the Wind*.

In a letter to Thomas Dixon, written August 15, 1936, Margaret Mitchell, author of *Gone With the Wind*, acknowledged the influence of Dixon's novels on her famous book and movie. She wrote:

"Dear Mr. Dixon:

"Your letter of praise about *Gone With the Wind* was very exciting, and the news that you want to write a study of the book was even more exciting. . . .

"I was practically raised on your books, and love them very much. For many years I have had you on my conscience, and I suppose I might as well confess it now. When I was eleven years old I decided that I would dramatize your book, *The Traitor*—and dramatize it I did in six acts.

"I played the part of Steve because none of the little boys in the neighborhood would lower themselves to play a part whereby they had to 'kiss any little ol' girl.' The clansmen were recruited from the small fry of the neighborhood, their ages ranging from five to eight. They were dressed in shirts of their fathers, with the shirt tails bobbed off. I had my troubles with the clansmen, as after Act 2, they went on strike demanding a ten cent wage instead of a five cent one. Then, too, just as I was about to be hanged, two of the clansmen had to go to the bathroom, necessitating a dreadful stage wait which made the audience scream with delight, but which mortified me intensely.

"My mother was out of town at the time. On her return, she and my father, a lawyer, gave me a long lecture on infringements of copyrights. They gave me such a lecture that for years afterward I expected Mr. Thomas Dixon to sue me for a million dollars, and I have had a great respect for copyrights ever since then.

"Thank you for your praise. Coming from a Southerner, and a Southerner of your literary reputation, it made me very happy.

"Sincerely,

"Margaret Mitchell"

9

WE DREAM

OF A REMAKE

David Wark Griffith

The twelve reel *Birth of a Nation* picture, which is still news in the press, is filled, as is *Gone With the Wind,* with the adventure as well as the bitterness and the problems of the Civil War. The first part of the movie, the original "colossal," has many thrilling war scenes interspersed with a couple of North-South love sequences.

Grim as the battle scenes are, the second part of the *Birth* is even more starkly gripping. It shows the sociological and emotional strains of the Reconstruction Era, with its accentuated racial conflicts, often spurred by Northern carpetbaggers who used freed Negroes as their agents. In some instances, too, there were Southerners who collaborated with Northern carpetbaggers for mutual profit.

The one man whose sense of justice could have given a more orderly direction to the Reconstruction Era was Abraham Lincoln. But Honest Abe was dead, slain by a fanatic— and those who hated the South soon won control of her government and people. "The South is a conquered land," said Austin Stoneman. "She must bear the price of her folly."

In this time of confusion arose a rebellious legion—the white-robed Ku Klux Klan— based, Thomas Dixon said, upon the clans of Scotland. The Southern Klan rode at night and its nocturnal bugle calls and quick actions chilled the blood of law-abiding and renegade Negroes alike.

Of such historical material—David Griffith employed four historians to check background facts—was the *Birth of a Nation* fashioned by a master director.

Because both were Southerners, Griffith and Dixon were deeply sympathetic to the problems of the South. She had fought nobly and well in the Civil War, and she had many wounds to bind. When these two men, one the most brilliant movie director of the time, and the other a fiery preacher, playwright, and Southern patriot, met and talked in our New York apartment, they generated a white hot enthusiasm to portray in the *Birth of a Nation* the tortuous rebirth of their beloved homeland.

I know this, because Harry and I, a couple of Northerners from Wisconsin, entertained both Griffith and Dixon many times. We sat with them for hours discussing the financing, the producing, the showing of this great movie which surpassed all our expectations.

It has been said by many critics, including minority groups, that the *Birth of a Nation* was conceived principally as racial propaganda. I do not believe this. Griffith, Dixon, Harry and I, who were closest to this picture from its inception, looked upon it solely as dramatic entertainment. And this is what it has proved to be for half a century.

Remember, if you will, that the villains in the photoplay, as well as in the novels on which it was based, were influential white congressional leaders, unscrupulous white carpetbaggers and easily led Negroes. Racial bias? Neither white nor black is lily-pure, nor ever will be.

In the years following the *Birth's* greatest box office earnings, 1915-1927, Harry and I had always thought that someday the movie could be remade and reissued profitably. So did Griffith and Dixon. Heaven knows all of us needed the money after some lean years. In the 1930's, '40's and '50's we tried many times to interest capital in such a project. Often we seemed to be on the brink of success, but eventually the deals did not go through. Would-be investors, prodded by militant minority groups, became increasingly wary about

Knickerbocker Theater, New York, 1915.

the *Birth's* controversial racial issues. They seemed to lose sight of the fact that the picture is dramatic entertainment, which is something many of the movies shown today are not.

Now, in April 1954, as Harry finished talking with Phil Ryan about a remake of the *Birth,* I turned off the television set in our Waukesha home. "Well, Harry," I managed to say, "perhaps this is it! Three-quarters of a million dollars for our rights to the *Birth* after all these years. I can hardly believe it!"

He found his voice. "Neither can I. But you and I always had faith in the movie, Roy. So did Griffith and Dixon. Too bad they are both dead and can't share in the new picture. But their heirs can. Ryan and his backers will want to bargain on the final price. We'll have to hang tight to get what we want."

I made a pot of coffee. Excitedly, Harry and I talked for hours about our many experiences with the *Birth,* our worries when we had tried to finance it, our jubilation when it became a smash hit, and our dejection when censorship battles arose and minority group opposition plagued the picture.

We talked also about our early days in the theater business when we started a string of nickelodeons in Chicago in 1905 on $100 which we borrowed from a friend. We were a couple of young fellows, fresh off a Wisconsin farm. But we were ambitious and not afraid of work. The same can be said of Adolph Zukor, Carl Laemmle, Sam Goldwyn, William Fox, and Louis Mayer. We became

Harry (right), at age 8, and me, at age 6. Taken on the farm in Wisconsin.

Owen Moore, first husband of Mary Pickford.

well acquainted with these men, for they got their feet wet in the movie industry at the same time we did.

We battled with these shrewd businessmen for movie star contracts, for scripts by prominent authors, and for theater sites. Because we were audacious and willing to take risks they would not take, we were temporarily ahead in the movie magnate parade—at least until 1916—and we achieved this position with very little capital.

In 1911 we formed the Majestic Film Company, principally to produce pictures starring Mary Pickford and Owen Moore. On our Majestic and Reliance Film Company payrolls at one time were Douglas Fairbanks, Lillian and Dorothy Gish, Mae Marsh, Bessie Love, Charles Chaplin, Gloria Swanson, Wallace Beery, Mabel Normand, William Hart, Blanche Sweet, Fatty Arbuckle, Ben Turpin, as well as many other players who later became famous. Practically all these stars got their start with us.

Our directors were the greatest in the industry in that 1911-1918 era—David W. Griffith, Thomas Ince, and Mack Sennett. And a young fellow named Raoul Walsh was on our payroll, too.

Harry and I had the difficult task of raising the money to finance all the movies which these brilliant directors were eager to make. It was a tremendous task to get capital, because at that time movies were generally regarded as a fad and a cheap form of entertainment which had no future. And who wanted to risk hard money on a passing fad?

"The movies have a future," Harry said to all who would listen. "Give us time to improve!"

Harry and I were among the first motion picture executives to interest Wall Street in the movies as a profit-making enterprise. Crawford Livingston and Felix Kahn, well-known New York bankers, were persuaded by Harry to buy some stock in our Majestic Film Company and to accept posts on the board of directors.

Majestic was the company that carried Griffith's contract, and Harry, as Majestic's president, engineered the deal.

"Zukor offered D. W. more money," Harry once told me, "but he signed with us for less because he knew we would let him experiment with little interference."

And let me say now that I believe the *Birth of a Nation* would not have been produced—at least for many years—had it not been for the wisdom, courage and financial ability of my brother Harry. Certainly Frank Woods wrote a fine photoplay from Dixon's novels and Griffith directed the movie masterfully. But both Griffith and Dixon were discouraged and thought the picture could not be filmed when the Majestic Film Company board of directors turned down the idea. But Harry pumped financial blood into the picture, because he believed in it, in Griffith and in Dixon. And it was Harry who sold others on investing the money Griffith asked for, so that production on the epic could begin.

"I'm going to bed, Harry," I said at two o'clock when the coffee pot was almost empty. "I'm very tired."

"I'm not," replied Harry, deep in an easy chair. "I'll just sit here awhile and think."

That attitude was so characteristic of Harry. He was a visionary, but he also knew how to plan. Laemmle, Zukor, Mayer, Goldwyn and others realized that. They paid him the tribute of following many of his policies. They started making long pictures after the *Birth of a Nation* became a financial hit. They launched their own film exchange groups and their own foreign representation when ours proved successful. They began to advertise nationally in the *Saturday Evening Post* and in other magazines, as we had long been doing, to show the public that the motion picture had come of age and now rivalled the stage for dramatic entertainment. But even while they followed his footsteps, Laemmle, Zukor and other producers lagged behind Harry at the time—especially in showmanship. They excelled him, however, in one important category. They topped him in shrewd management.

Once having made a financial success of a picture, they were conservative enough to stop and consolidate their gains before moving into new and larger production programs.

Harry didn't and perhaps couldn't consolidate. He was continually brimming over with ideas to develop the movie industry—and these ideas drove him. I often urged him to proceed more slowly, but he wouldn't listen. Once he had a plan for a new movie com-

pany or picture or program, he would propose to put it into action as soon as possible, using whatever available cash his various companies could spare.

He would then work feverishly night and day to finance his projects by securing loans, or by selling stock. He was a sincere, earnest, and persuasive man.

This was the way Harry organized Majestic Film Company, Mutual Film Corporation, Epoch Producing Corporation and Triangle Film Company, all important movie organizations in their day. He almost became a movie magnate of vast power and influence with the success of the *Birth of a Nation,* but his weakness for immediate expansion helped bring about his downfall in 1918. So did his troubles with his trio of famous directors, Griffith, Ince, and Sennett.

And now in April 1954, Harry and I were going to meet with Phil Ryan in Milwaukee to discuss a full-scale remake of the *Birth of a Nation.* There was a chance we might receive up to a million dollars for our interest in this old but very much alive silent motion picture. We could use the money!

No wonder I had difficulty going to sleep that night.

Scene from Bill Hart's "Hartville."

RYAN

GETS AN OPTION

Lee's Surrender
(from **Birth of a Nation**).

A few troublesome points developed when Harry and I met Phil Ryan of the Thal Syndicate at the historic Plankinton Hotel in Milwaukee, to negotiate on the proposed remake of the *Birth of a Nation*. Ryan, a short, stocky man and an enthusiastic talker, had recently seen several private showings of the *Birth* and was quite impressed with its remake possibilities.

However, he quickly pointed out something which Harry and I already knew. Our Majestic Film Company to which Thomas Dixon had sold movie rights in 1913 for production of the *Birth of a Nation* from his novels *The Clansman* and *The Leopard's Spots,* apparently bought only the silent picture rights. Epoch Producing Corporation (a firm which Harry and I also controlled, and which bought the *Birth* from our Majestic Film Company in 1915) did put a sound track on the silent film in 1930 with Dixon's signed consent and also Griffith's.

But now that Thal Syndicate wished to produce an entirely new movie, based in part on the previous *Birth* picture, their executives felt that they wanted to purchase not only the Aitken interest in the *Birth* story and title, but also felt they needed a contract with Thomas Dixon's widow for whatever rights she might have in the old as well as in a new *Birth* movie.

Ryan said that if we would give him an option on our rights in the picture, then he would proceed to contact Mrs. Dixon in North Carolina to try to get an option from her. Armed with these two important options he felt certain that Thal Syndicate and its

backers would then be ready to complete final purchase arrangements.

We argued and bargained for quite a while during lunch and also later up in Ryan's room. Finally Harry said wearily, "All right, we'll give you an option on our rights, based on our percentage of stock ownership in the picture. We want Mrs. Dixon to get a fair share, too."

So a nominal option price was agreed upon and paid to us. A pleased Ryan left for Hollywood a few hours later, after assuring us he would contact Mrs. Dixon as soon as possible and let us know when he completed arrangements with her.

"Well," Harry said as we drove back to Waukesha, twenty-five miles distant, late that warm afternoon, "we may not get seven hundred fifty thousand dollars as we expected, but we should get a half million or more, if this purchase is completed. How would that suit you, Roy?"

"A half million," I said with a smile. "Think we could spend that at our age, Harry? After all, we're in our seventies."

Harry turned his twinkling eyes upon me, but he didn't answer.

We heard from Ryan only sporadically in the months that followed. It seemed that negotiations with Dixon's widow were prolonged because of price considerations, and this caused final production plans to move slowly.

Then one day Harry and I were startled to read in *Film Daily,* authoritative motion picture trade magazine, the following headline and story under a Hollywood dateline, December 2, 1954:

"BIRTH REMAKE SET BY THAL SYNDICATE

"Plans to remake the *Birth of a Nation* as the most lavish spectacle ever filmed, were completed when all rights to the property were acquired by the new Hollywood syndicate headed by financier, Ted Thal, who is president of Thalco, an affiliate of TEMA Corp. Also in the syndicate is Michael Spack, president of TEMA.

"Based on the thinking that a new generation of movie goers offers the story a potential gross of between 50 and 60 million dollars, the group plans to devote $8,000,-000 to production.

"Original *Birth* was produced and directed in 1915 by D. W. Griffith and heads all time box office roll with total grosses in excess of $50,000,000.

"Acquisition rights to property were acquired at a cost of more than $750,000, after eight months of negotiations with Harry E. Aitken, president of the old Epoch Producing Corp. which owned title rights, and the widow of Thomas Dixon who owned rights to Dixon's historical novel, *The Clansman*. Deal for transfer to the new group was completed by Phil Ryan, spokesman for the group.

"Ryan said that Thal group plans remake of the *Birth* in color, with a cast of some 15,000 soldiers, and that discussions already have been started to secure the Todd AO process, along with Cinemascope for its production. Thal intends to offer the *Birth* as a roadshow attraction in keeping with the scope and immensity of subject.

"Discussions have already taken place with Dudley Nichols to write the screenplay. No release date has been discussed with any of the major studios, but group has already been approached and upon the return of Thal, now in the East, talks have been scheduled with two major studio heads, Ryan said. Production will not begin until men of top caliber are secured to handle production and directorial reins."

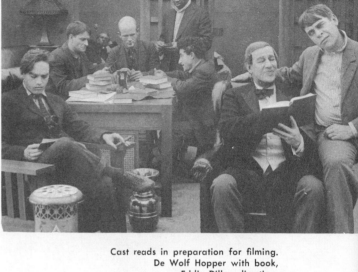

Cast reads in preparation for filming.
De Wolf Hopper with book,
Eddie Dillon directing.

There was one glaring error in that news story, of course. Harry and I had not been paid in full for our rights to the *Birth of a Nation*. All we had received was option money. We also assumed that neither had Mrs. Dixon been paid in full. Undoubtedly someone at Thal had goofed on the details of that news story—or there had been a leak.

But Thal had some responsible men behind it, and so Harry and I had good reason to believe that production of the remake would shortly proceed, as the *Film Daily* article seemed to predict. Which could also mean that we would soon get the rest of the money due us.

Mae Marsh and Robert Harron
in a scene from Triangle's
Hoodoo Ann.

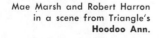

Administration building,
Culver City Studio.

Louella Parsons, noted columnist, had this to say:

"*The Birth of a Nation* will be remade—wow! After eight months of negotiations with Harry E. Aitken who owned the title rights, and the widow of Thomas Dixon who wrote *The Clansman* on which the historic film was based, Thal Syndicate paid $750,000 for rights to make a new *Birth* picture."

Walter Winchell wrote:

"The plan to remake the *Birth of a Nation* should be deplored. The original exploited bigotry. Why dig up something that deserves to be buried?"

Inez Robb stated:

"It takes gall to remake the *Birth of a Nation*. Even in this crazy mixed up world, some things are sacred. They can be tampered with only at grave risk to the tamperers.

"This is just by way of warning, and not too friendly at that, to a brash Hollywood syndicate now planning to remake *Birth of a Nation*. I regard this as unmitigated gall.

"Anything most people do, someone else eventually can do better. But I do not believe this Hollywood syndicate headed by Phil A. Ryan can improve on the original D. W. Griffith epic. I don't think they can come within a mile of it.

"There is a fine old axiom 'leave well enough alone,' and Mr. Ryan and his syndicate ought to paste that in their hats, and then tip their lids every time the name of Griffith, the maestro, is mentioned."

Hardly foreseen by Thal, apparently, was the nationwide avalanche of publicity which followed the *Film Daily* article. Much of the publicity was extremely controversial.

Heading the list was a blast by telegram which Roy Wilkins, administrator for the National Association for the Advancement of Colored People, sent to Thal Syndicate. *Variety* reported the telegram as follows:

"Mr. Wilkins stated that his organization was as uncompromisingly opposed to this film today as it was when the picture was first released in 1915. He said that the announcement of a new version was of 'deep concern' to the group and others who know of the great damage the original version did in slandering the entire Negro American population through its naked incitement to racial hatred and violence.

" 'The revival of the unashamed and undisguised racial animosities of the era in the middle of the twentieth century following two wars and unparalleled progress in race relations can do little except to inflame the uninformed. The new film version of this inflammatory film cannot escape being regarded as an effort on the part of some group or groups to encourage the 1876 rather than the 1955 view of Negroes as American citizens, and as a roadblock to the orderly and just attainment of rights.' "

Executive offices,
Culver City Studio.

Variety, December 8, 1954, reported the proposed remake thus:

"Projected remake of David W. Griffith's 1915 feature, the *Birth of a Nation* by a Hollywood syndicate headed by financier Ted Thal has been greeted in New York film circles with plenty of surprise and consternation. Proposed deal ties the original Thomas Dixon *The Clansman* and the title and rights of the *Birth,* now owned by Harry E. Aitken, into one package.

"What causes New York film men to shake their heads is fear of the social and political consequences to the motion picture industry inherent in a revival of an old controversial classic in which hatred and prejudice against Negroes was as open as was admiration and approval of the Ku Klux Klan.

"New York curiosity centers on Dudley Nichols' ideas. He is the man who is mentioned to make the 1955 shooting script. How does he intend to handle the obsessive theme of the negro—raping—white girl which Dixon and Griffith repeatedly stressed?"

Triangle Studio's property room.

Columnist Land in the same issue of *Variety,* using the headline "Bedsheets Are Poison!" said:

"Immediate repercussion to news that a Coast syndicate will remake the *Birth of a Nation* has been consternation and dismay on the part of negro leaders and considerable headshaking among whites (see separate story) who recall the brutal subject matter of Thomas Dixon's two novels, *The Clansman* and *The Leopard's Spots* upon which D. W. Griffith made his controversial classic.

"Producer Phil Ryan from Hollywood has already made the only answer possible at this moment when the shooting script is not yet written: 'Critics should hold their fire until they know they have cause to criticize' or words to that effect. Without explicit disclaimer of using the Ku Klux Klan night rider stuff, or the rape scenes which were obsessive with Griffith, the implication of Ryan's comment is that the 1955 *Birth of a Nation* will be an historic panorama a la *Gone With The Wind.*

"On sober second thought it seems fairly evident that no picture can possibly dare, at this late date, to glorify the thoroughly discredited Ku Klux Klan which was— let it not be forgotten—also against Catholics and Jews. Too wide a segment of the population would be offended. Sheer economic self interest dictates that the new shooting script must bear little or no resemblance to Griffith's.

"Nor can it be overlooked that America's 15,000,000 Negroes today are a respected and courted five billion dollar market. And big filmgoers. On top of all these economic factors, there is, of course, the factor of morality and social responsibility.

"Thus the reaction of the negro community, while understandable, is perhaps, as Ryan suggests, premature.

"Common sense will not allow open hatrio-

teering such as was possible in 1915. Griffith's picture was not only a great money maker, but also a great mischief maker, and it is as plain as anything can be plain that the story treatment of 40 years ago simply could not get a production code seal today, nor get by the censorships of the states—surely not in New York.

"However, clamor against the idea will continue until the Thal Syndicate thinks through its story line and makes it clear to the socially minded elements of the country that no glorification of night riders and no antagonism to negroes is the intention. When that aspect has been taken care of, then it can perhaps be argued that the *Birth of a Nation* is an established presold title, its choice for a remake is not without showmanship."

Joseph Henabery as Abraham Lincoln,
in **Birth of a Nation.**

We are PROTESTING this movie
BECAUSE
  • IT ENCOURAGES RACE HATRED!
  • IT GLORIFIES LYNCHING OF
          NEGROES!
  • IT APPROVES OF THE KKK

WE KNOW THAT EVERYONE WHO BELIEVES IN
AMERICAN DEMOCRATIC PRINCIPLES WILL NOT
SUPPORT THESE THEORIES!

  EVERY ADMISSION FEE paid to SEE
  "Birth of a Nation" ENCOURAGES the
  making of more anti-democratic
  films!

SUPPORT DEMOCRACY AND EQUALITY
    STAY OUTSIDE

Issued by: P R O G R E S S I V E   P A R T Y — 56th A.D. CLUB
R. Lovell, Chairman —— B. Edelman, Treasurer
2960 West 8th Street, Los Angeles - DRexel 5 2 1 1
PHONE YOUR PROTEST TO THE MANAGER AT WAlnut 1103

W. Ward Marsh of the *Cleveland Plain Dealer,* December 16, 1954, a drama critic who helped to promote the showing of the *Birth of a Nation* in some cities back in 1915-16, wrote:

"The stirred up hornet's nest which has resulted from the announcement of the remake of the *Birth of a Nation* is inevitable, premature, and needless.

"In the first place, if the scholarly Dudley Nichols is going to do the script for this big screen version, all of us may rest assured that Nichols is not going to do what Griffith did.

"This embittered Southerner struck hard at the Negro. Years later, he tried to apologize for his wrong with that death scene on the World War I battleground in *Hearts of the World,* but he had done his damage with the original.

"*Birth of a Nation* is, even today, a powerful and inflammatory film. The original *Birth* is still dynamite, and I will fight with my last word to prevent its revival for public showing.

"But this does not mean that I oppose a new version. There is still a magnificent story in the Civil War and the rebirth of the country to be told without the introduction of hate and racial prejudice which so colored the Griffith version.

"Whatever the *Birth of a Nation* was—and believe me its power today has not been lessened much by time—it was also the greatest political football the screen has ever furnished.

"It has swayed elections, created judges, elected at least one governor, defeated many others for how many offices no single individual knows, nor does any one person know what else it has done.

"I hope for very good reason that the *Birth of a Nation* has been resold and that Dudley Nichols and his associates remake it. A new version may finally enter the Griffith version, which, in these days of racial anxieties and stress, must be forgotten."

Poster typical of many used
to protest showing of film.

18

Harry and I were not discouraged by all this adverse publicity. It was old stuff to us, a continuation of the controversy which the picture aroused back in 1915 and which had continued throughout the years.

In 1922 when Harry and I were fighting censorship proceedings in Chicago, a young opposition lawyer, employed by the city in the case, met Harry in the hall after a particularly torrid court session.

The lawyer slapped Harry on the back. "Best damn picture I ever saw!" the honest lawyer confided.

His name was Harold Ickes.

In early 1955 the controversial publicity about the Thal Syndicate's *Birth* remake project still appeared frequently in newspapers, trade journals and movie magazines. In addition, minority group pamphlets were circulated against the showing of the picture. From this barrage of publicity, some pro but mostly con, one important fact began to emerge: if a new *Birth* were to be made—at an estimated investment of $8,000,000 or more—a watered down version of the old silent movie would be necessary for modern box office appeal. And this was apparently what Thal Syndicate had in mind.

Phil Ryan had many problems to face before the new *Birth of a Nation* could get into production. His Thal Syndicate apparently had enough financial backing to produce and pro-

mote the new picture, but its executives who had talked with major studio heads, declared that experts felt that only a script writer such as Dudley Nichols could write an acceptable photoplay for a remake on the controversial *Birth* picture.

Nichols was as busy as an interpreter at a United Nations meeting and could not be pinned down to contract a work date on the new photoplay.

Even armed with an acceptable photoplay, Ryan would have to contract a major studio willing to tackle the big production job for Thal Syndicate and assign a top flight director to the film.

Whether such a rewritten version, diluting the racial drama and soft pedalling the fiery Ku Klux Klan of the original *Birth* film, would have enough box office appeal to become another colossal was a gamble which the energetic Thal group apparently still thought was worth taking.

So, for the time being, there was nothing for Harry and me to do except nurse our option agreement and hope that all details would eventually work out. We could also hope that once the new picture got into actual production, we could go to Hollywood and watch operations—and incidentally arrange to be on hand to collect the money still due us. It was a prospect very pleasant to think about.

Hartville Ranch Studio in Santa Monica Mountains.

WHEN HARRY
SIGNED GRIFFITH

The Little Colonel (Henry Walthall) stands poised atop the Confederate trenches.

The *Birth of a Nation* story actually began in 1911 when Harry and I organized the Majestic Film Company, our first important producing firm. Two of the budding stars we signed to make pictures—taking them away from Carl Laemmle—were petite, flaxen-haired Mary Pickford and her handsome husband, Owen Moore.

Previously Harry and I had been engaged in organizing and operating film exchanges in Milwaukee, Chicago, St. Louis, and other cities. We bucked the "film trust." When it cut off the supply of films to us because we had dared to make a two reel experimental film on our own about the James Brothers, we found ourselves very short of pictures to supply our customers—theater owners.

Of course, we were able to buy some films from a few independent producers, but that supply was not enough to keep all our exchanges in business. So we had to look elsewhere for additional films, and we thought of England and France where some very good pictures were being made.

"Let's go to Europe and look things over, Roy," Harry suggested one day. "We can take along some old American films to rent to European exchanges, and perhaps rent European films for our exchanges in the States."

Within a couple of weeks we were in London gathering information about the film market in the European area. The result was that we set up a foreign distributing company named Western Import Limited, and I was installed as manager. At the time there were only one or two small film sales agencies in London, and so I found a ready market for the old films we had brought along. Later, as business increased, we opened branch offices in Paris, Berlin, Copenhagen, Rome, and other cities. All of these connections I supervised from London. Film buyers from Japan, India and Australia coming to London for films also found their way to our offices.

"Look for quality pictures and comedies, Roy," Harry said just before he left for his return trip to the United States. "I know the people back home expect this infant industry to improve."

Western Import Limited prospered from the start. We booked many European films for showing in the United States, and in turn also booked many American films for showing in other countries. But within six months we realized that if we wished to keep pace with the fast moving picture industry we would need to produce pictures, too.

That was why we organized Majestic Film Company and shortly thereafter bought a controlling interest in Reliance Film Company (another producing company) from Charlie Baumann and Adam and Charlie Kessel, owners of the New York Motion Picture Corporation with whom we were destined to have many years of fine business relations.

These were excellent moves on our part, for within two years our Majestic and Reliance companies were producing and distributing numerous one and two reel features and had enough stature in the industry so that Harry was able to sign a very promising director from Biograph. This director's name was David W. Griffith. His dreams about four reel and even longer pictures were too visionary for the conservative-minded Biograph board of directors, and so Griffith came with us.

Adolph Zukor wanted Griffith in his employ. In his recent book, Mr. Zukor stated that he offered Griffith $50,000 per year to become a director in his company. But Griffith signed with Majestic for a much smaller salary—$300 a week, plus stock.

Why? One reason was that Harry offered Griffith a financial interest in Majestic Film Company, plus an interest in some of the movies he was to direct. Biograph apparently had not been willing to use such incentives to hold Griffith. And apparently Zukor had not considered this important inducement in his drive to assemble the largest motion picture company of the time.

This "sharing of opportunity" in picture making under Majestic and with Harry, gave Griffith what he had long wanted. It opened the way for him to propose and develop his ideas for special pictures, some more than five reels.

I recall that I made a trip to New York from London late in 1913 to talk with Harry about foreign film office expansion. It was then that he told me the details of the transaction whereby Griffith signed a Majestic contract, and of the program the director had in mind.

On that trip I brought back with me from London a new yellow Leon Bollee automobile. I loved sporty cars. Now that I had a sizable income—in keeping with the expanding volume of business done by Western Import Limited—I felt I could afford a snappy foreign car.

Actually, the Leon Bollee was the second of three foreign cars I was to acquire within a few years. A year earlier I had brought over a Renault. Next year it would be à Rolls Royce.

The stevedores were unloading my yellow Bollee with the green leather seats when my brother rushed up to greet me at a New York dock.

He shook my hand warmly. "Welcome home, Roy. I've got wonderful news. Griffith's pictures are drawing well. We were lucky to sign him—"

"Take it easy," I cautioned a stevedore. "Don't get those fenders greasy."

Harry's attention swung to the shining yellow car. "Is that yours?"

I nodded proudly. "Like it?"

"Beautiful. Now I *know* Western Import is making a profit. And you are wearing better clothes than last trip. Why, you look like an English lord, Roy. A big improvement over the suits you wore when you came off the farm not so many years ago."

We both laughed heartily. "There are many things I admire about the English, Harry," I said. "They may seem to be stuffy people, but they have fine taste and have a steady, sobering sense of values. In our position as aspiring movie executives, we must dress and live the part. Our apartment and English butler are part of the plan. So are our foreign cars. They're fine advertising for us in New York."

Seated in my Renault
in front of
Western Import, 1911.

Bobby Vernon and Gloria Swanson in Keystone film, **Teddy at the Throttle.**

"You've always insisted on this kind of front, Roy, and perhaps you're right. Back in our film exchange days, our electric car in St. Louis impressed theater owners. So did our fur coats and stiff hats. You were always the social type, but that's important, too. I suppose I'm too serious. Anyway, you and I make a good team."

I was glad Harry said that. I felt the same way. Out of the corner of my eye, I nervously watched the stevedores move the dismantled crating from the area where my shining Leon Bollee car stood. "Harry," I said, "tell me about Griffith. I've seen some of his Biograph pictures in London, including the long one, *Judith of Bethulia*. He is certainly doing some daring camera work. It adds to the drama of his pictures."

"Don't tell him I said so," Harry smiled, "but I think the fellow is a genius. He wasn't satisfied at Biograph. They wanted him to stick to making short pictures and he was anxious to make longer features. He knows we are willing to try to improve movie quality and have a lot to offer him."

"How much did you offer him?"

Harry was very serious. "Three hundred dollars per week in cash, plus the outright gift of four hundred shares of Majestic stock, valued at a hundred dollars a share."

I whistled.

"I had to," Harry defended. "Zukor baited him with a thousand dollars per week. What I offered Griffith topped Zukor's offer, because Griffith and I—under terms of the Majestic contract—can also make two special pictures of our own each year, and split the profits."

"Does Griffith know we have very little available capital and an oversupply of nerve?" I asked drily.

"I think he likes our nerve," Harry laughed. "He believes Majestic is going to grow, because we have an eye to the future. And we've done all right to date, Roy. Griffith plans to grow with us. That's something he couldn't do at Biograph. Every time I meet him he starts to tell me about an exciting Civil War story he'd like to make from a book written by Thomas Dixon, an author and a Baptist preacher. Griffith wants to make it into a long motion picture and give it highly dramatic treatment."

"I'm very anxious to meet him, Harry. Everyone I know connected with the film business thinks Griffith has a great deal of talent."

Harry chuckled. "You *will* meet him—tonight. He's in town for a week from our California studio. Dixon and he are coming to dinner at the apartment. You'll probably hear all about that Civil War story. It's like a fever with both Griffith and Dixon. All they need is money—and they think I can furnish that."

"Money!" I grumbled. "That's always been our trouble. People with capital don't have faith in the future of the movies. But you did get Crawford Livingston and Felix Kahn of Wall Street to buy a little Majestic stock, I've heard."

Harry nodded. "Yes, I got acquainted with them at the Waldorf—an after-dinner lobby episode. Later we dined often. Before we moved Griffith to California, I took Kahn and Livingston to the Broadway loft—a former rug factory—where D. W. was filming some scenes from the *Battle of the Sexes*. Kahn and Livingston were impressed. They stayed two hours. And they bought a little Majestic stock. I have hopes they'll buy more. We need their support."

I was impressed. "Would they perhaps be the first Wall Street bankers who have actually put money into the movies?"

"I believe so. And if we handle them right —who knows? Now how about driving that sporty Bollee to the apartment? It's a wonderful day to show it off along Broadway."

"I'd like to," I smiled. "I'd have suggested it, if you hadn't."

On the way to the apartment, Harry told me that he had been worried somewhat by the liberal contract he had given Griffith, but thought it would work out profitably.

"Griffith has promised me he won't interrupt Majestic's regular program pictures of two four-reelers per week," Harry said. "He'll work in the Griffith-Aitken specials piecemeal during production breaks. I don't see how a man can make two types of pictures at one time. But I had to sign him on those terms, or lose him."

"You said he was a genius."

"Yes, I did, and I'll have to let him try to prove it. I'm a partner in his two annual special pictures. As president of Majestic I had to insist on this. It's the only way I'll have power to hold him down. I am beginning to suspect he could be somewhat of a spendthrift when it comes to his own pictures where there is no set budget as there is on our Majestic program features."

"Temperamental, is he?"

Harry growled. "Isn't everyone in this movie business? Griffith has a lot of ideas burning him up. We'll have to wear seven league boots to keep up with him. This Civil War picture idea he has may be too big for us to handle now, especially from a financial angle. But we've got to hear him and Dixon out tonight. I've been stalling them, waiting to get you in on the deal."

Douglas Fairbanks and Seena Owen in early picture made for Majestic Film Co.

Fine Arts Studio at Hollywood and Sunset Blvd., where Griffith made **Birth of a Nation** and where Douglas Fairbanks made his first twelve pictures for Majestic. Later owned by Columbia Pictures; the studio burned several years ago.

That Civil War picture that Griffith had in mind was really big enough for any movie producer to handle. It was the *Birth of a Nation*. Practically any director or producer or banker in those days would have loved to have had a financial interest in that picture— after it became a top box office hit. But none of them had the type of foresight required back in 1913-1914.

No one, you see, not even Griffith, nor Thomas Dixon, nor Harry nor I, dreamed that the *Birth of a Nation* would become the most famous motion picture ever produced, and that it would hit a financial gross which would make the entire movie industry gasp. No one dreamed either, that it would become the most controversial motion picture of all time.

I MEET GRIFFITH

AND DIXON

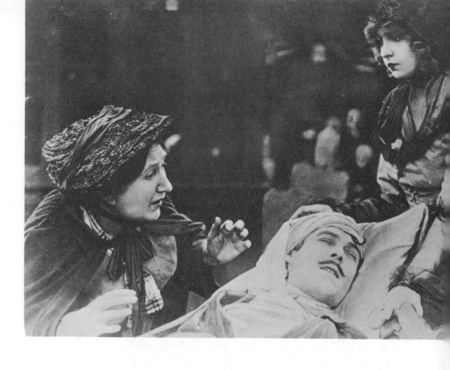

Colonel Ben Cameron (Henry Walthall)
lies wounded in Northern hospital,
where his mother (Josephine Crowell)
visits him. Elsie Stoneman
(Lillian Gish) looks on.

Griffith and Dixon came to our apartment for dinner that night. Both were tall and handsome men. Griffith's reserve impressed me immediately. I noticed his stiff bearing and his hypnotic dark eyes. Dixon, on the other hand, was florid and energetic. He had a ready smile, and his blue eyes were very friendly.

"D. W. and Tom," Harry said genially, "I'd like to have you meet my brother Roy. He just got in today from our London office. You should see the sporty Leon Bollee car he brought along."

I felt Griffith's swift appraising glance, saw him inspecting my smartly tailored English suit, and the scrutiny made me feel a little uncomfortable.

"I feel I already know you," Dixon smiled. "Harry has told us so much about you."

"And I have heard a great deal about you, Mr. Dixon, and your books and the play *The Clansman*," I said warmly. I turned to Griffith. "Your pictures are very well received in London and Paris, Mr. Griffith. Especially *Judith of Bethulia*."

Griffith barely smiled. It was evident he was pleased, but he still was taciturn and had a sort of "wait and see" attitude.

An excellent meal of roast lamb was served by our precise English butler, Dunstan, and his wife, Nellie. Harry, Dixon, and Griffith questioned me at some length about London and Paris, and the kinds of films being produced there. They listened eagerly while I told them about film buyers, audience reactions, and the scarcity of good motion pictures to meet the demand of Europeans.

Griffith commented on my English clothes and politely inquired the name of my London haberdasher. I noted that he wrote the name and address in a small black-covered notebook.

This admiration for things English, I learned, resulted in Griffith visiting my London haberdasher several years later. The haberdasher, I was told, made many suits for Griffith.

In fact, my experiences in England, and my description of English life, seemed to hold considerable fascination for Griffith. Although he maintained his polite reserve, he wanted to hear about my weekly trips to the English countryside, my views of London theaters, and the celebrities I had met. I believe that my English reminiscences opened the door to my friendship with Griffith, which was to continue for many years.

Friendship of a sort, that is. No one could completely break through that Griffith aloofness. Perhaps that is why he never had any close friends. But I have seen Griffith as relaxed, perhaps, as anyone. He liked to accompany me when I dined out with feminine friends. And he loved to dance.

"Any dine and dance routines tonight, Roy?" he would sometimes ask me after a difficult screening day.

We often spent evenings together. One time when he came to New York for a conference he was especially interested in meeting some models I had told him about. These girls were members of Lucille's troupe. She was a famous English modiste, and I had met some of her models on one of my boat trips from London to New York.

Griffith and I took two of these models to dinner one night at a colorful New York restaurant and we danced for two hours or more. When I drove Griffith back to his hotel later, he was as gay and smiling as I have ever seen him.

But now—in our apartment with Harry, Dixon, and me—Griffith looked slightly impatient. We lighted cigars and Harry turned to Griffith. "As you know, D. W., Roy is my partner in many movie companies and film exchanges. I'd like to have you tell him about that Civil War movie you want to make from Tom's books and play."

Griffith seemed surprised that Harry placed so much confidence in my opinion. I could see that he realized for the first time that he was dealing with a brother team, not just one man, and that this knowledge would play a part in his presentation.

There was magnetic intensity in the man's dark eyes as he turned his attention upon me. There are many who have said that Griffith had hypnotic power. I believe it, for I felt myself fascinated under his gaze. Dixon, resting easily in a chair near Griffith, had the appearance of an intent and pleased author who hears someone else passionately recite a work which he has created.

Griffith gave a graphic presentation of his proposed epic. "The real story of the Reconstruction Era has never been filmed," he said in a deep voice. "It offers great possibilities for exciting drama and extensive camera techniques. Tom is a Southerner. He knows how deeply the South was hurt and how long it took her to regain her strength. I, too, am a Southerner. My father was a Confederate officer. I know the hardships the Southerners endured in defeat."

He went on reciting the high points of Dixon's story. "But," he said finally, "it would take ten or twelve reels to tell such a story effectively."

"Twelve reels!" I exclaimed. "That would be an entire evening's performance. Most of the pictures I have been handling in London and through our Berlin and Paris offices are two reelers."

Griffith smiled a little coldly. "The first movies were one reelers. But we are now up to four and five reel pictures. People are ready for longer pictures, if the story is dramatic. In my Civil War film, there will need to be many prewar and war scenes. I have some new ideas for showing battle action. All this will take footage. Then the Reconstruction Era will require much space. We must lay emphasis upon the revengeful congressmen and senators, and upon the unscrupulous, white carpetbaggers. We must show them bent on revenge and plunder, stirring up the free Negroes, confusing them and creating misery and suffering among the Southerners. Then we must have many Klan scenes."

"Ah, the Klan!" spoke Dixon suddenly. "It was the Klan that saved the South!"

"The Civil War is known to all children and adults," Griffith explained. "Our picture would have nation wide appeal if we can highlight the drama, especially the battle and Klan scenes."

Harry and I asked many questions. Wouldn't the cost of the picture be prohibitive, especially in the face of an untried market? Would theater owners schedule such a long picture— some of them were still reluctant to handle four and five reelers. Would the making of the picture interfere with the production of other program films Griffith was making for our Majestic and Reliance companies? Griffith was under contract to produce at least two regular program pictures for us per week. We needed that many to keep our film exchange and exhibitors supplied.

Griffith was not discouraged. "I can keep on schedule with those program films. Don't worry about that. And we can work longer hours to make *The Clansman*. I can use many of the Majestic actors and actresses at very little additional pay. I've got some promising ones, lovely Lillian and Dorothy Gish, a sweet girl named Mae Marsh, and a fellow named Henry Walthall. This *Clansman* picture will be worth a hundred of the other movies!"

Harry, who had heard Griffith detail his Civil War picture plans on previous occasions, watched for my reaction to Griffith's project. "Your contract with Majestic, D. W. gives you the privilege of producing two special pictures per year of your own choosing," he said, as though summing up the situation for me, "and in these specials I am your financial partner. We are allowed to use Majestic facilities and stars so long as the production does not interfere with production of regular program films. The special picture is to be billed to you and me at cost, plus ten percent. This *Clansman* will be such a special, won't it?"

"Yes. And this picture is going to cost a great deal to produce. I look to you, Harry, and you, Roy, to get the money together for this production. Surely you can get it from Majestic, Reliance or Mutual, or from Wall Street?"

Harry smiled wanly. He knew how difficult it was to get investor money in a new and untried industry. "How much do you think you would need to produce the picture?"

We looked at Griffith, who was frowning. "I believe it can be done for about forty thousand dollars," he said finally. "I'll do my best to hold costs down."

I caught my breath. Forty thousand dollars! As far as I knew no other motion picture made to date in the United States had cost more than ten thousand. Many were produced for about one thousand dollars per reel.

"And Tom, how much would you want for the film rights to *The Clansman* and part of the *Leopard's Spots*?" asked Harry tensely.

Thomas Dixon smiled. He straightened in his chair, uncrossed his legs and leaned forward. "I know money is tight," he said genially, "and I know it will cost a lot to produce the picture. I will settle for twenty-five thousand cash!"

All of us were silent for a moment. The making of the film would cost forty thousand dollars and the photoplay would bring expenses to sixty-five thousand, an unheard-of sum in motion picture circles for one film production in those days. I think the size of that figure dampened our spirits a little.

Then Harry said, "Gentlemen, sixty-five thousand dollars is a very big sum to raise for one picture. But I suppose it could be done, if we decide to go ahead with the filming of *The Clansman*. This industry won't stand still, even for us. We've got to look toward the future and anticipate great things."

I could see that Harry had committed himself. He apparently was sold on the movie even if it ran to twelve reels. And yet he would not give Griffith and Dixon a definite answer until he had consulted me privately. He was summing up for me how he felt about the picture that was so close to Griffith's heart.

Griffith's eyes were shining. One reason he had signed a contract with Majestic Film Company was because he felt that Harry and he were kindred souls in a sense. Harry was a wizard in raising money, and Griffith was a top-notch director, with dreams of the future. Both had hopes of a brilliant future for the motion picture industry, and a secure place for them in it. Both were visionaries and sometimes inclined to take a gamble on the strength of their convictions. Often they were impatient at any slowing in the execution of their ideas.

"If we decide to produce the picture," Harry said finally, "our immediate step will be to get the financing. Our Majestic and Reliance Companies, as you know, D. W., as well as Mutual Film Corporation, our distribution agency, are sending approximately sixty thousand dollars per week to Hollywood. Some of this money is allocated to you for Fine Arts Studio productions; some goes to Thomas Ince for Bill Hart Westerns, and some goes to Mack Sennett to produce the Keystone Cop comedies. It's no easy matter to get all that money together every week. Roy and I and others have had to forego our salaries sometimes to make certain our directors got their budget money on time."

"I appreciate that," said Griffith, "but if anyone can raise money for *The Clansman*, you and Roy can do it, Harry. You know the right people and can persuade them. And this *Clansman* picture could make a great deal of money for all of us. I'm certain of it."

Harry smiled. "Well, we've got bankers Felix Kahn and Crawford Livingston on our Mutual and Majestic boards now," he conceded. "They bought a small amount of stock. How far they'll go in backing us for production of a big special Civil War picture is another matter. They carry a lot of weight on the boards of both companies. And they are hard-headed business men."

"Not so hard-headed but what the glamor of the movies appeals to them," pointed out Griffith. "When you brought Kahn and Livingston over to our loft on Broadway six months or so ago to see us filming those pot boilers, I saw Livingston grin when he spotted those dancing chorus girls. Both Kahn and he stayed about two hours, didn't they?"

"Yes," Harry laughed, "but they'll act different across a bargaining table, perhaps. I want to talk this over with Roy tonight, D. W. If we decide to finance this picture, I'll call a meeting of the Majestic board and put it up to them, and see if they will participate."

It was past midnight when Griffith and Dixon left the apartment. All of us, even Griffith, were quite excited. It was as if we knew that great events awaited us.

"I'll call you before noon and let you know what Roy and I decide to do," Harry promised Griffith.

Griffith turned to me. His eyes were friendlier than when he had asked me about my

Seated in my Rolls-Royce.

experiences in England. "When do I get a ride in that fancy yellow Leon Bollee automobile?" he chided. "I'll only be in New York another five days."

"Tomorrow, if you wish," I said. "We can tour New York. I am eager to see the sights again. And I want to see if the girls here are still as beautiful as those I met in London and Paris."

Griffith's eyebrows lifted, as though he saw something about me he had not noticed before. "They *are* just as beautiful," he said earnestly. "I'll be glad to point out some special beauties to you. And when you come to Fine Arts Studios in Hollywood, you can take a close look at some of the stars whose salaries you and Harry pay."

So he likes women, I thought. I must remember that. Harry is the thinker, always full of ideas and plans for development. Griffith likes that quality in him. But Harry is no social type, and Griffith apparently likes a little fun now and then.

I knew that in a partnership such as existed between Harry and me, one of the Aitkens would have to shake a lot of hands, exchange pleasantries, listen to confidences at dinner tables, or while dancing—or while toasting with a glass of champagne. That's part of building a movie empire too, and I liked that part of my job quite well.

"How about you, Mr. Dixon?" I smiled. "Want to see New York with us tomorrow?"

Dixon laughed and shook his head. "Not this time, thank you. How would a preacher look sitting in the back seat of that yellow sports car with you two waving at all the pretty girls along Fifth Avenue? Besides, I'm to be a guest speaker Sunday. I've got a sermon to write."

THE DECISION

Warren O'Brien, Waukesha photographer, left, and my brother Harry on my right, in the 1950's when the three of us produced a Wisconsin historical film.

At breakfast the next morning Harry and I talked about Griffith's Civil War picture. "Now that you have slept on the idea, Roy, how does D. W.'s project strike you?" Harry asked, buttering some toast and adding the delicious English marmalade I had brought with me.

"It's a daring idea, all right. I have no doubt that Griffith can make an interesting picture with any material he chooses. We *might* make a lot of money on *The Clansman*. But ten to twelve reels! I'm afraid of it. Will people sit that long in a theater to see one movie?"

"Griffith says they will. And I'm inclined to believe him. This picture isn't for a nickelodeon or a cheap theater, Roy. It's got to get bookings at big, legitimate stage theaters. And at top prices!"

I chuckled. "And with many people buying tickets, too, if we're to pay the heavy production costs. I've heard that Griffith is inclined to be a little extravagant. But if you are willing to assume the risk of making this picture, I suppose we can manage to raise the money somehow. We've always found the finances for other film projects so far. Perhaps our luck will continue."

This brought a smile from Harry. "I knew you'd decided for the picture when you said good night to Griffith, Roy. But I wanted you to get a good night's sleep before I asked you for your answer."

"How about you, Harry? Is your mind made up?"

"Partly," he came back, sipping the last of his coffee. "This is a tremendous venture for us, and it could be the turning point in our careers, Roy. I'm going to talk it over with Charles Brown."

Charles Brown was a devout Christian Scientist who had experienced a marvelous healing through his religious belief. Harry had met the man at a community event, was impressed with him, and Brown and he had become friends. It was a relationship which was to last for many years, and it affected both Harry's life and mine.

While he was not a member of the Christian Science Church, Harry was an admirer of the principles of the sect, and he often consulted Brown about business and personal problems. I doubt if Harry would have made any important decision without talking it over with this slender, cheerful Mr. Brown. He had great confidence in the man's advice and in his closeness to divine presence.

Much of the vision and daring attributed to Harry and to me came from Harry's faith in the words of advice and encouragement of Mr. Brown. The man often told Harry that God gave him these ideas and opportunities in his chosen field, and that Harry should have unlimited faith in God and try to fulfill his ideas when they appeared reasonably feasible.

And Harry was the type of man who, although strong in his own convictions, still felt he needed a greater power to guide him. Brown frequently told Harry that there was but one mind, one intelligence in the universe, and that Harry could rely on this mind to guide him through the difficulties of this great new movie industry. This faith Harry carried with him to his death. A banker once wrote of Harry, "He inspired his associates with his philosophy and beautiful sentiments."

"I wish that this decision about *The Clansman* and its big production expense could be postponed for six months or a year, Roy," complained Harry as he prepared to leave for Brown's office. "Then perhaps we'd have more time to cash in on Tom Ince's Bill Hart Westerns and Mack Sennett's Keystone comedies with Charles Chaplin, in addition to the films Griffith will produce. But I will see what Brown has to say about the Civil War venture."

After Harry had gone, I called Griffith at his hotel and found him eager for the tour in the Leon Bollee. I went to our garage and found Matt Hosley, the chauffeur we'd brought from Waukesha, already polishing and fondling the yellow automobile.

"Oh, it's a fine automobile, Mr. Roy," Matt exulted, his blue eyes glistening.

I knew Matt expected to drive even though he was not yet really familiar with the car, so I told him to take me to Griffith's hotel.

Griffith was waiting in the hotel lobby. He seemed a little reserved again, but the moment he spotted the Yellow Bollee at the curb he smiled. "The French have an eye for smart design, haven't they? Any more cars like this in New York?"

"I hardly think so," I said. "Probably not this color, at least."

"Good," Griffith smiled. "I wonder how many of our friends will see us as we cruise on Fifth Avenue." Then, "Has Harry any news for me?"

"Not yet. We are to meet him at the apartment for lunch."

Griffith and I spent a gay hour and a half touring downtown New York that sunny fall morning. People, including many pretty girls, stared at us, and we stared back at some of them. We went up and down Fifth Avenue, to the East River, through Central Park, and later back to the apartment.

"Well," chided Griffith, "how about the girls? Do they compare with those you've seen in London and Paris?"

"I think so," I chuckled. "But I can't be certain until I get a closer look."

Griffith, sitting stiff backed in the Leon Bollee beside me, turned his head in my direction, a twinkle in his eyes. "I see," he said, and I felt him appraising me. "You're different from Harry, aren't you? He likes to sit and think for hours. Perhaps you're the one who can help him have fun occasionally. He needs it. And I do, too."

I looked at Griffith and smiled. "I'm getting hungry. Let's go up to the apartment."

Harry answered the sound of the door buzzer. There was a smile on his lean face and a glow in his eyes. "Brown counseled me to go ahead, Roy!" he said confidently. "Opportunities may not wait. I've called a meeting of Majestic directors for ten tomorrow morning, D. W."

"Wonderful!" Griffith reached for Harry's hand and shook it vigorously. It was a moment of elation between men, who, having made a decision, share their exuberance in extreme good-fellowship. When Harry and Griffith got tired of shaking each other's hands, they began shaking mine. All of us felt very happy.

"Come," said Harry. "This calls for a little wine!"

We toasted and did a lot of talking. There was so much to do, so much to discuss. Finally, it was decided that Griffith and Dixon were to come to lunch at the apartment the next day, following the Majestic board meeting. Harry expected the meeting to end at noon, and then he would join us.

Griffith and Dixon, eager to hear from Harry that Majestic would finance the producing of *The Clansman,* arrived at our apartment at 11:30 a.m. We talked of the beautiful fall weather, the plays on Broadway, my Leon Bollee car, but all of us knew this conversation was just to mark time. We were all nervous; it seemed we could hardly wait until Harry came back with the good news. Then we would celebrate with luncheon, a little wine and more talk of great plans.

Miriam Cooper and Elmer Clifton in
The Artist's Wife.

Mildred Harris, first wife of Charlie Chaplin, in an early Aitken picture.

Seena Owen, who played in many Triangle-Ince productions, co-starred with William S. Hart and others.

The moment the apartment door opened and I saw Harry's wan face, I knew something had gone wrong. Wearily, Harry put his hat on top of the player piano. "Well, gentlemen," he said sadly, "the Majestic board turned us down. They won't advance the money to film *The Clansman*. Even Kahn and Livingston advised against the picture. I had counted somewhat on them to help me convince the others. They said the picture would cost too much. It would be too big a risk. We should stick to the two to four reelers."

Griffith and Dixon, who sat on a big davenport, turned to stare unbelievingly at each other. Griffith seemed to sag, and the usually energetic Dixon was at a loss for words, unusual for such a voluble preacher.

Finally Griffith said, "How about Mutual, your distribution company, Harry? You are president of that, too!"

Harry shook his head slowly. "Mutual's board is loaded with Majestic directors, too. We'd get the same answer. Kahn told me so."

Now Griffith seemed a little desperate. "Can't you find *someone* who will back this picture, Harry? You've raised money to launch Majestic and Mutual and to buy Reliance. It seems so easy for *you!*"

Dixon looked anxiously at Harry, too, and I could see that both of these men hoped he could accomplish a financing miracle, despite the turndown by the Majestic board. But at the moment our resources were committed. Surely Griffith and Dixon knew that.

What now of Brown's advice, I thought?

Would Harry accept defeat? Was this project of Griffith's too big for us to handle?

"Well, gentlemen," Harry said quietly, "I'm hungry, and I imagine you are too. I'm sure Dunstan has prepared for us. Let's eat."

Celery soup, shrimp salads, parfaits and coffee helped to lighten the atmosphere somewhat, especially for Harry. As he looked up from his coffee, there was determination in his face.

"Don't look so discouraged, D. W.," Harry said, slowly putting away his napkin. "I suppose Roy and I can *try* to raise the money. In fact," his face took on a stubborn expression, "we *will* raise it! At least enough of the forty thousand dollars to get the picture started. The rest can come later—somehow."

Paul Powell, Constance Talmadge, and Mary H. O'Connor in an early Triangle-Fine Arts picture.

Griffith's head lifted quickly, and the disappointment left his eyes. "I *know* you and Roy can do it, Harry!" he said huskily. "Dixon, we are not whipped yet. This picture will be an epic, and we'll all make money on it!"

Harry turned to Thomas Dixon. "Tom, I don't see how we can raise cash to pay you twenty-five thousand dollars for the film rights now. How about a twenty-five percent royalty interest in the movie, with a two thousand dollar down payment in advance one of these days?"

Dixon looked startled. Plainly he had not expected this. Apparently he hoped Harry would offer to raise twenty-five thousand dollars for photoplay rights. He stared across the table unseeingly, with that straight ahead look some men have when in deep thought.

"I'd rather have the cash," he said slowly. "I'd counted on it for certain obligations I have. But, if there is no other way, I suppose I could take a twenty-five percent royalty interest for my pay and hope to Heaven I'll make something out of it."

Thomas Dixon did make something out of it. Something in the neighborhood of three-quarters of a million dollars over a twenty year period. It was the best investment he ever made. How exasperated he would have been had he accepted $25,000 cash for film rights for the *Birth of a Nation*. It is true that $25,000 was a whopper of a price for photoplays in 1913-14 when seventy-five to a hundred twenty-five dollars was considered a fair sum for two to four reel scripts. And who dreamed that twenty-five percent royalty interest in a movie would grow into a fortune?

Now that we had decided to put *The Clansman* into production, Griffith, Harry, and I began talking earnestly about what would be needed in the way of special equipment for the picture, and which had to be paid for immediately, and which could have deferred payment dates.

Dixon sat listening to our discussions and smiled amusedly. His work was done; he had written the books and the stage play from which the photoplay would be adapted by Frank Woods, our top scenario writer. All Dixon could do was to hope that Griffith and the Aitkens could make a motion picture which the public would clamor to see, so that he and all others associated with the venture could collect large royalties and dividends.

When Griffith and Dixon departed by taxi a few hours later, I said to Harry, "What made you promise to raise that money, despite the Majestic turndown? Was it Brown?"

Harry nodded confidently. "Remember, Roy, we never know what is waiting for us if we have faith. We can't pass up opportunity, or someone else will beat us. We've got to see this movie through!"

And that is how it was that the responsibility for obtaining the money to finance *The Clansman*, later named the *Birth of a Nation*, fell upon the shoulders of a couple of young men not many years out of the Wisconsin farmlands, and whose financial resources were already stretched perilously thin over several film producing companies, a distribution company, a foreign film chain, and a number of film exchanges.

One wrong, ill-advised step and—

WE SEEK

FINANCING

Spottiswoode Aiken and Lillian Gish
in **Souls Triumphant.**

To understand the difficulty of raising money to finance motion pictures in the period 1910-1915, one needs to keep in mind the rather low degree in which the movies were regarded as a cultural influence. Practically the only enthusiasts for the new form of entertainment were working men and their families who patronized the poorly ventilated nickelodeons or the equally musty second-rate theaters. Even Griffith, prior to the success of the *Birth of a Nation,* was ashamed of the films which he and other producers brought to the screen.

Wall Street and other investors, casting profit-inquiring glances at promising American industries, could see no monetary future in motion pictures as a steady source of sizable dividends. Investors generally smiled amusedly and turned away when movie producers begged for capital.

It is true that Felix Kahn and Crawford Livingston bought some Majestic Film Company and Mutual Film Corporation stock at Harry's suggestion and accepted positions on the boards of both companies. But these men were intrigued by the glamor and excitement of the movies, rather than by the thought of profits. Being on the boards of two film companies gave them the prestige of being able to visit our New York and Hollywood studios where they could view our feminine stars at close range. These bankers loved the gay dining and dancing parties that film people held almost constantly after working hours.

I watched Kahn and Livingston many times at such parties. I saw their eyes twinkle with amusement and interest at the carefree talk and antics of film people at hours when astute bankers are generally thought to be asleep.

"Kahn and Livingston are not going to risk any more than token investments," I once told Harry. "They are getting a thrill being on the board of a newly organized film company, but they are keeping their hands on their pocketbooks. It's like a vacation close to home for them, to be on the inside of such a queer industry."

"But the longer they keep their stock and stay on the boards, the more interested they'll become," Harry predicted with a knowing smile.

At this time, too, there were few firmly established movie producers. Adolph Zukor, Carl Laemmle, William Fox, and Sam Goldwyn were experiencing financial ups and downs. Their companies were no larger than ours, and they also had to rely on current picture receipts to keep afloat financially. Louis Mayer, who later attained the heights as a movie producer, had not yet established his reputation. He was to accumulate his first million dollars as a distributor of the *Birth of a Nation* in New England.

"Well, Roy," Harry said cheerfully the morning after Griffith had departed for Hollywood, "this is the day we begin to try to raise the money for Griffith's epic. I've got forty-two people on my list to call on. How many have you?"

"I'm not so well known as you. I've only

got twenty-seven. I've been in London almost two years. I'll have to start getting acquainted all over again in New York."

I do not claim that we engaged in the biggest search for money in the infant movie industry that cold fall of 1913, but it looked like a very formidable job to us, when we considered our other commitments. And that is exactly what it proved to be.

Of course, we maintained our rather luxurious apartment on West Fifty-seventh Street and our English butler and his wife. Matt Hosely, our chauffeur, was also on our payroll. Harry and I dressed well, and many influential people who saw Matt driving us about New York in the unique, yellow Leon Bollee identified the owners as the prospering Aitken brothers who owned several film companies, including many film exchanges, including a European branch, and who had under contract the promising director David W. Griffith with his bevy of budding stars, including the Gish sisters, Mae Marsh, Henry Walthall and many others.

Rich? We certainly were not. Our finances were stretched to the breaking point by the demands of our fast expanding operations. In fact, our finances had been stretched thin ever since we started in the movie business in 1905. Events always moved so fast that we frequently had to look hard to find extra money somewhere to take advantage of one exciting opportunity after another.

But the exterior appearance of being prosperous—even though we were not—was very important in our business. It inspired confidence and gave us the reputation of being bold movie magnates who were going somewhere and challenging others to keep pace with us.

Offhand, it would seem a small task to raise $40,000 to pay production costs for D. W. Griffith's special picture *The Clansman*. Actually, Harry and I confidently expected we would have little trouble in raising the money within a few weeks—particularly if we really worked hard at it.

We began visiting more frequently at such places as the Hotel Algonquin, the Waldorf Astoria, numerous theatrical offices and other places. Here we met many friends and also made new friendships. Bankers often dined

with us at our expense, introduced us to some of their business friends who usually inquired about that curious business in which we were engaged—the movies.

We found ample opportunity on such occasions to mention our super Civil War picture, soon to get into production on the West Coast in our Fine Arts Studio under David W. Griffith. We also indicated quite clearly that there was an opportunity for a few far-sighted persons to invest in such a picture on a syndicate basis and perhaps reap sizeable profits if the picture became a success.

Earlier in our producing career, in order to make the meager finances of our two film production companies stretch—Majestic and Reliance—Harry had organized syndicates for some of the pictures our companies produced. One of these pictures was *The Battle of the Sexes*, in which Lillian Gish appeared.

Under the syndicate plan, Harry would visit his friends and business associates and sell them an interest in one movie at a time. He would, of course, retain controlling interest in each picture for Majestic or Reliance in his own name. Then, when the picture was adequately financed and produced, and the profits arrived at, they were distributed *pro rata* among syndicate stockholders.

By use of a syndicate, a film company could get additional capital for production of pictures. Its own capital, therefore, could be used sparingly and "stretched" over more pictures. Through the syndicate method, too, many a cautious investor who might not wish to buy stock in a motion picture company, could take a non-crippling flier in a limited way on one picture.

Other film companies often financed pictures through the syndicate plan, too.

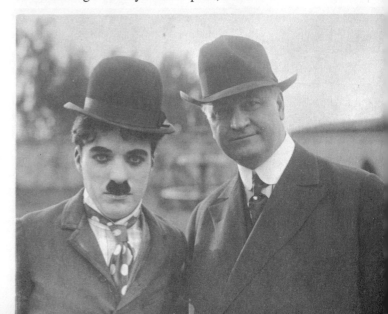

Charlie Chaplin and John R. Freuler.

Mary Boland in **The Edge of the Abyss.**

Harry and I tried to form a syndicate to finance *The Clansman* and we worked hard at it for several weeks. One night at the apartment after Dunstan and his wife had retired, Harry said, "I can't figure it out, Roy. This is the most difficult picture I have ever tried to finance. My syndicate prospects shy away from it."

"I know," I replied gloomily. "Forty thousand is too much for a single picture. A ten to twelve reeler is too long and might be a box office flop, I'm told. Besides, who is interested in the Civil War? It happened so long ago, and too many books have been written about it. Those are the opinions that my prospects have thrown at me. 'Nice of you to offer to let me in on this picture, Roy, but I think I'll pass this one up, if you don't mind.'"

Harry smiled a little bitterly. "Exactly. And word has gotten around that the Majestic

Charlie Chaplin in **Dough and Dynamite,** which was directed by Mack Sennett.

board turned down the project. That doesn't help us. My friends are afraid of this picture. They think we're gambling too much on it. But we gave Griffith our word. We've got to raise the money somewhere!"

I looked glum.

A sigh escaped Harry's lips. "There *is* a way, Roy, but I was hoping it wouldn't come to this."

I made no answer. I thought I knew what Harry would say.

"I'm president of Majestic, of Reliance, of Mutual, of Thanhouser," Harry said. "You are an officer in these companies, too, and also of Western Import. We receive weekly salaries from each. We can earmark twenty or thirty percent of these salaries toward *The Clansman* fund. For weeks, if need be."

"But we have other obligations!" I protested quickly. "This apartment, Dunstan and Nellie, Matt, food. And the Leon Bollee won't run on water."

"I know," Harry said patiently, "but we *can* get some money from ourselves—the hard way."

I said nothing.

"We own stock in these companies, too. Felix Kahn will give me a loan on that stock —the part of it which isn't already held by him on other loans."

I snorted, "And if Griffith's picture is a flop, where will we be with mortgaged stock and still under obligation to raise the money every week to send to Griffith, Ince, and Sennett on the Coast for regular program picture production? Harry, maybe we got into something that we had better get out of as quickly as we can."

"Why, Roy," Harry reproved, "this is no time to get faint-hearted. We've already taken many risks since we got into this business through nickelodeons in Chicago."

"So we have, but my heart hasn't improved because of these constant risks. Let's phone Griffith and see if he can postpone the picture."

Harry was shocked. "D. W. phoned me this afternoon asking for money. He has already scheduled production of the picture. He has rented land to shoot battle scenes. He has placed orders for mules and horses and many other needed items."

I jumped to my feet angrily. "That's the

Bobby Harron and a bevy of gay, silent-day stars.

trouble with this business, Harry. Everyone seems to want to move so damn fast. What's the hurry? We hardly get time to handle one problem and along comes another urgent one. When can we settle down and consolidate this business, and build some reserves?"

"I don't know," sighed Harry. "If we stop too long to catch our breath someone else will get ahead of us and seize the initiative. You can bet your last film that Carl Laemmle, Adolph Zukor, and Sam Goldwyn are not taking things easy. They're up nights, too, trying to figure out which moves to make next."

The telephone rang and Harry answered. "Oh, hello, Tom . . . Yes, I suppose so . . .if it must be. Sure, I've got a copy of the contract here. Roy is with me. . . . We'll wait for you. . . ."

Harry walked back to the window where I stood looking out into the autumn night. "That was Tom Dixon. He wants to read the contract once more before he signs . . . and he wants a two thousand dollar advance now. He's got some obligations to meet."

"Who hasn't?" I growled. "Have you got two thousand dollars?"

"Not at the moment. But it's Friday. I'll give Dixon a check and the money will be in the bank Monday."

"Where'll you get it?"

"Our salary checks come in tomorrow. They'll help. Besides, a few of the business-

men who turned me down on the syndicate financing indicated they might lend me some money for the picture on my *personal* note."

I turned quickly. "But that would place an undue risk on you, Harry, if *The Clansman* fails. It means your friends know that if the picture fails on the syndicate plan, they would lose their investments. But if they lend *you* money on a personal note—and the picture fails—they know you will repay them sometime. You're that kind!"

Harry looked at me calmly. "Of course, I am. I'll have to risk those personal loans, Roy. Are we still in this special picture together with Griffith, or does one of us back out now?"

"Well, if you are so confounded confident that the risk is worth taking, and that *The Clansman* will be a success, I'll go along," I said reluctantly. "We've almost been smashed financially so many other times, I suppose I can stand one more siege of the jitters."

Harry looked relieved and we shook hands. "I knew I could count on you, Roy," he said quietly.

The doorbell rang. "That must be Dixon," Harry said. "He got here in a hurry, didn't he? I wouldn't have to give him the two thousand dollars advance now. The contract can't be signed until our lawyers hold a meeting. But Tom needs the money."

Harry felt his left back pocket. "Yes, I've got my checkbook," he muttered. "What a wonderful thing credit is."

THE MONEY
IS SENT
TO GRIFFITH

Alma Rubens, a Triangle player.

So Dixon was appeased temporarily with a $2,000 payment. This plus his contract guarantee of twenty-five percent royalty, was all we could offer at the moment. While Dixon regarded this agreement as a compromise from his original demand of $25,000, it turned out to be the best contract he ever made.

In the years which followed, Thomas Dixon earned almost a million dollars in royalties from the *Birth,* enabling him to live like a Southern gentleman in North Carolina, where he became a land speculator. He even formed a motion picture company called the National Drama Corporation and began producing movies. He wrote the *Fall of a Nation* and it was directed by Hartley Cushing. Victor Herbert was engaged to write the music for the movie, and he also conducted the orchestra at the Liberty Theater, New York, on opening night, June 6, 1916. But the *Fall of a Nation* was a box office flop and Dixon went back to North Carolina to speculate in land and to wait for more *Birth of a Nation* royalty checks.

Few people know that Dixon wrote a second *Birth of a Nation* photoplay in 1936 which Harry, Griffith and Dixon planned to use in a remake of the famous film; but they were unable to raise the money for such a venture. Harry told me several times that he had paid Dixon for this second photoplay out of his own funds.

Now, in mid-1914, Harry wired Griffith at our Fine Arts Studio in Hollywood that $25,000 had been raised and that this sum was available for his use through Majestic Film Company.

"I didn't want to organize a separate company to produce this special picture," Harry said to me, "so I turned the money over to Majestic to handle for us, and I obtained in return Majestic stock for twenty-five thousand dollars."

Since Harry was president of Majestic, he had no difficulty in making such an arrangement. The Majestic board, which had dodged the financing of the special picture, agreed to Harry's idea of routing the $25,000 in special funds through the company. It was the board's way of being agreeable to Harry so long as none of Majestic's regular funds were tied up in the Griffith special.

But there was risk. Through the arrangement, Majestic temporarily owned the picture, although Harry and I held additional stock. Could we, I wondered, take over ownership when the *Birth* was completed and showing in theaters? I hoped so.

Griffith was enthusiastic. He wired that he would increase the hours needed to film the long picture, but he hinted that his ideas on scenes, costumes and techniques were constantly expanding, and that we should try to raise the remaining $15,000 we had promised and send it to him. He had a feeling he would need it rather soon.

"He receives twenty-five thousand dollars credit and immediately asks for more," grumbled Harry. "He should know how we sweat blood to raise that money. Griffith is a brilliant fellow, but we've got to hold him down, Roy, or he'll break us."

To try to keep news about a new motion picture quiet was almost impossible. Word began to seep back to New York from Hollywood that Griffith was very excited about his spectacular and had likened it to an epic. There were rumors about new camera techniques, or improvement in presenting material; talk about expanded flashbacks, closeups, soft focus, fade outs, long shots, and night photography; unconfirmed tales of projected battle scenes involving hundreds of extras hired as Union and Confederate soldiers. Newspaper reports also stated that Griffith rehearsed some scenes twenty times, so insistent was he upon getting action exactly as he wanted it.

The picture was not titled *Birth of a Nation* until after its Los Angeles premiere, February 8, 1915. While it was being filmed, the picture was named after the book from which it was taken, *The Clansman.*

"I like Griffith's enthusiasm," said Harry one day as we lunched at the Hotel Algonquin, "but does he realize how quickly twenty-five thousand dollars and more will vanish in this sort of spending program? Rehearsing scenes so many times! Think of the added cost for that sort of thing. Roy, have we got a tiger by the tail?"

"I hope not," I answered. "Mack Sennett and Tom Ince are clamoring for more money all the time, too. We send them about twenty-five thousand dollars a week, or a hundred thousand a month for their productions. I wake up nights dreaming that hands, hands, hands are always outstretched for money."

Harry laughed as he laid his napkin on the

Mack Sennett, one of the great Triangle directors.

table. "Majestic and Reliance standard two to four reel pictures are grossing well at theater box offices, thank heaven. And our exchanges are growing rapidly and getting more customers. We may have our troubles financing this fast-growing empire of ours, Roy, but so long as Griffith, Ince, and Sennett are producing pictures that will pull people into the theaters, we'll manage somehow."

"The trade has it that Tom Ince and Sennett are envious of Griffith," I said. "They probably feel that if the Aitkens are handing out large sums for spectaculars they want more to spend on their pictures, too."

Harry smiled. "Certainly. And I like that type of rivalry. It brings out the best in all these men—and means better pictures, too. This eventually means more money for us, Roy. But we hold the reins. And we can pull them tight when we have to."

One day in late summer Harry looked glum when he came back to the apartment for dinner. Even Dunstan and Nellie's excellently prepared roast lamb didn't bring him cheer. I thought I knew what was wrong. In Europe an archduke had been murdered. There were hot tempers and finally two giants, Germany and the Allies, glowered at each other. War seemed inevitable.

"It could involve all Europe," Harry said slowly, "and perhaps this country, too. Such a conflict will be terrible for the world and for movies too. Foreign film production will be cut drastically, and we need foreign films to give variety to our programs."

"But American films will sell abroad, if we can make enough of them. Even in wartime people need diversion."

Fatty Arbuckle and his wife, Mina Durfee.

"When you go back to London in about three weeks, be sure to check closely on the situation and cable me," Harry said. "We must watch trends very carefully."

By the end of the following week Harry and I had raised another $15,000 to bolster the filming of Griffith's epic. Investors who earlier had hesitated to put up money for the picture now had heard the promising news about it, and some were willing to open their purses and take a flier. Griffith now had $40,-000 total credit assigned to his picture through Majestic, but much of it, of course, had already been used.

One day Harry said, "Roy, before you go back to London, you and I had better take a trip to Hollywood to see Griffith and talk over the expense of this epic picture. I want to see a breakdown on costs. Besides, we can visit Sennett and Ince, too, and check on their plans and listen to their troubles."

We took the long railroad ride to Los Angeles where we registered at the Alexandria Hotel, which was also Griffith's home at the time. A few hours later, clad in our best English cut clothes, we procured a studio car and set out for the Fine Arts location on Hollywood and Sunset Boulevards.

As we drove along, I could not help feeling that it was our hard earned money which was giving Griffith the opportunity to use his talents the way he wanted. And he was entitled to the glory received, for talent is talent. For our part, however, Harry and I wanted something, too—profits for the money we had invested; and assurance that it would be spent as wisely as possible in this unpredictable movie business.

Several years ago when I visited Lillian and Dorothy Gish and had tea with them and Anita Loos at the lovely Gish apartment in New York, they asked me to tell them about the early days of the movies.

These beautiful stars knew that Harry and I had been in the "flickers" for many years before the girls began to work for Griffith at Biograph. As I related how Harry and I were always scrambling to earn and borrow money to finance our growing movie enterprises, Lillian Gish, who is still as beautiful and charming as she was in the days when she played the part of Elsie Stoneman in the *Birth of a Nation*, gasped.

"Why, Roy," she said. "I never suspected you weren't rich. When you and your brother came to the Fine Arts studio that first time, Dorothy and I were quite awed. We were young in the show business, and we peeked around the sets of the studio trying to get a glimpse of you. Mr. Griffith had pictured you and Harry as big, prosperous New York bankers on whom our jobs depended."

I laughed. Lillian, Dorothy, and Anita were still more amazed when I told them that Harry and I had deliberately spent more money on clothes, foreign cars, a fine apartment, butler, and chauffeur, than prudence dictated—all for a necessary effect on others.

There was considerable coolness between Griffith and us that day at Fine Arts studio. There is always coolness between people who have sharp differences on matters vital to each. But after a few minutes of talk, Griffith began to warm a little. He started to tell us about his epic and his eyes shone. It was evident he was wrapped up in what he considered to be his masterpiece.

"Don't worry, Harry," he said. "I'm making the regular Majestic and Reliance standard pictures on schedule and supervising the work of our five sub-directors on the lot. I always manage to find a few hours a day, too, to work on *The Clansman,* on which I am using some of the Majestic actors and actresses. So, you see, we *are* cutting corners."

This was promising news.

"You can tour the lot and see some films in production right now," Griffith invited. "And this afternoon we'll shoot a *Clansman* scene. Then tonight we'll go over some cost sheets."

Harry and I exchanged glances. Neither of us said anything. Griffith seemed willing to talk business with us. Or did he sense a gleam in our eyes which told him to be diplomatic and agreeable at this time to those who were furnishing the money?

The short, stocky genius, Billy Bitzer, was the cameraman that afternoon as he always was on a Griffith picture. Griffith used only one camera in shooting the *Birth* film—probably because of cost. That meant only one film negative was produced. Later, we often wished that we had had two cameramen, or more, shooting negatives. That one negative got excessive use. Nowadays studios have a half dozen or more cameramen shooting negatives on important pictures so that many negatives are available from which to make prints. If our one *Birth* negative had been lost or destroyed by fire—

Griffith directed the famous dance scene in the *Birth* the afternoon that Harry and I watched. A huge wooden platform had been erected for the ballroom scene. In costume were Lillian Gish, Miriam Cooper, Mae Marsh, Bobby Harron, Donald Crisp, Henry Walthall, Elmer Clifton, Raoul Walsh and many other soon-to-be famous movies stars performing under Griffith's expert guidance.

The scene showed the soldiers dancing with their sweethearts. Within a few hours these

Al St. John,
Triangle-Keystone star.

men would leave for war. Gaiety was mixed with sadness as the orchestra played dreamy waltzes. Griffith sat on a chair on the platform, a broad-brimmed hat shading his face, and in his hands he held a big megaphone. Now and then he shouted directions.

I must admit that I was thrilled watching Griffith as he directed the filming. The thought went through my mind that a couple of ex-farm boys like Harry and me had made this motion picture production possible, that our talent for organizing and promoting and raising money brought these gifted directors and players together to make entertaining pictures for millions. And I was proud to be a part of it.

I watched with interest as Griffith ordered Bitzer to film parts of the dance two or three times, until it was just the way the master wanted it. I saw Bitzer frown and knew he felt Griffith was being too particular. But Bitzer never argued with Griffith in public. Their private discussions, however, were often torrid.

Douglas Fairbanks in an early Triangle picture, shortly after he deserted the Broadway stage for a career in the movies.

From his platform spot Griffith looked over at Harry and me and smiled when the soldiers were kissing their sweethearts, mothers, and sisters goodbye. I knew he hoped we were pleased. Griffith's smile when a scene was well done will always remain with me. He was extremely charming when he was in a happy mood.

"The scenes are dramatic," Harry whispered to me. "Too bad they cost so much to film."

That night after a fine dinner at the Alexandria Hotel, Griffith took us to his room. We talked about the *Clansman* picture, and Griffith explained his costs. For the big battle scenes, he said, he needed many men as soldiers. Some had to be outfitted in blue and some in gray. And battle equipment was needed. Then there was the matter of horseflesh. Horses were high priced because the Allies were bidding for every good horse that could be found. But he had saved a little money, Griffith said. He had arranged to borrow some of Tom Ince's horses and cowboys for a few scenes. The cowboys would make excellent Klansmen, he indicated.

The next day Griffith was filming Klan scenes and he invited us to be present. I must admit that the hair on my head tingled as the hard-riding, white-robed Klansmen thundered by on sweat-streaked horses. After the picture was showing in theaters throughout the nation, many movie critics said that most Americans were stirred by the scenes of the swift-riding Klansmen.

In an old Epoch Producing Corporation release, I note one of our writers said, "Griffith loves best the field work when he can be in the open and direct big armies. G. W. Bitzer at the camera, Mr. Griffith at the megaphone, is the way it works out. A 100 h.p. automobile is used by the two' co-workers in taking the wild rides of the Ku Klux horsemen. Bitzer and Griffith travel directly ahead of the furious riding cavalry, with the camera's eye turned back upon those South Carolina cavaliers. It is a perilous but mighty fascinating job."

Another excerpt from a publicity release gives a glimpse of the working Griffith. "Griffith makes frequent across-the-continent trips every year. His business headquarters are in New York and his studios in Southern California.

"The four days across the country are not wasted. When preparing the *Birth of a Nation* he carried with him American histories and historical novels, a suitcase full. On other trips he takes along a dozen or more of the best sellers to see the kind of artistic fare the public is demanding. Still other times he loads up with Nietsche, Plato, and Maeterlinck.

"To understand Griffith you must realize his passion for accuracy of detail. He has the history as well as the imagination of a great historian. Nicolay, Hay, Tarbell, Herndon, Fleming, Dixon and many others were the raw material for his work. West Point graduates helped him with the strategy. National guardsmen with their officers and complete camp equipment, enlisted companies, regiments and brigades, were his soldiers. The director's aim was not merely to do a yardage of pictures, but to do it right.

"Imagine then, Griffith's army setting forth one morning upon Grant's campaign against Lee at Petersburg, Va. It is no hillside picnic, this expedition. The thousands of fighters—said to be 16,000—were used in the filming of the *Birth of a Nation,* are costumed, accoutred and armed in replica of the Civil War combatants. There is a long artillery train with old fashioned cannon and mortars of 1864; there are signal corps, ambulance corps, horse, foot, bridge builders, sappers and pioneers; in the rear rolls the slow moving baggage train, loaded with quartermaster supplies of food, cooking utensils and shelter. At night tents are pitched, wells dug, messes prepared. In three days' march the army reaches the wide valley selected as the battleground.

"Here one finds the salient features of the Petersburg field in 1864 reproduced. Griffith's location men, already on the ground, have had long lines of trenches built which stretch for miles. Here hummocky ground has been smoothed to the plain over which the cavalry charged; there a ravine is excavated or a hill is raised, from behind which masked batteries are to fire."

On that trip to Hollywood, Harry and I also visited Thomas Ince and Mack Sennett. We met tall, stern William S. Hart at the Ince studio. I liked Hart's deep interest in the old West, and his pictures were drawing well at the box office, attesting to his sincerity. Ince was making a steady stream of Westerns which were as popular an entertainment feature as Westerns are today.

At Mack Sennett's studio we encountered gaiety and slapstick comedy wherever we went. Soon we were surrounded by a bevy of beautiful, bright-eyed girls, including Mabel Normand, Gloria Swanson and Teddy Sampson. I liked the gay spirit of the Sennett studio and wished I could have stayed longer. A year later I did get back and I went swimming and dining quite often with Mabel Normand and Teddy Sampson. I wasn't so anxious to become a movie mogul that I couldn't take time to get to know these delightful, vivacious actresses.

Actually, Thomas Ince and Mack Sennett were working directly for the New York Motion Picture Corporation, owned by Charlie Bauman, and Adam and Charlie Kessel. But Majestic, Reliance, and Mutual Film Corporation—Harry's companies—had contracted to buy all of New York Motion Picture Corporation's productions and distribute them through Mutual. This naturally involved lending money to keep the Ince and Sennett studios operating regularly and gave us considerable control of policies. Later, in 1916, we bought New York Motion Picture Corporation from Bauman and the Kessels, but that is another story.

We met once more with Griffith before going back to New York. "The picture you are making from Dixon's novels is a stirring one," Harry told Griffith, "but it has already cost us more than any other picture we have ever made. Will we get our investment back?"

Griffith's dark eyes flashed. "This picture will be a classic, Harry. The public will love it. Tell investors what you have seen of it. Then perhaps they'll put up more money to complete the big scenes we still need in the picture."

So Griffith wanted more money. That didn't look too good to us. And Griffith was quite irritated because we talked so constantly about holding down costs. He wanted nothing to prevent him from making his epic the way he wanted it.

"Make the picture with the forty thousand dollars you already have," Harry told Griffith sternly as he bade us goodbye at the railroad station. "Right now we can't promise another nickel. We've got many other financial commitments. This isn't the only picture we are financing."

The last thing I noticed as the train began to pull out was the bitterness on Griffith's long face and the stern set of his jaw.

I sailed for London the following week. It was the seventh of the twenty-eight trips across the Atlantic that I was to make during our burgeoning movie career. Harry managed to see me off, although I knew he had a hundred more important things to do.

"Keep me informed on the film situation over there, Roy," he said seriously. "I intend to make another trip to Hollywood in a month or so. I want to see for myself how Griffith took our advice. Perhaps I can still help him cut a few corners on that picture."

We both laughed.

"You and Griffith are so much alike, Harry. You both like to take chances—each in his own way. It's strange to hear you say you're going to try to hold him down. You've seen eye to eye with Griffith on many things."

"D. W. and I are alike in some respects, but I have a slightly better business sense than he," Harry said. "Everyone says he is reckless with money. I don't want us to lose what we've got in that picture. It's my job to see that it doesn't sink you and me and hurt Majestic, Reliance and Mutual, too."

I knew what Harry meant. To go along with Griffith on his super picture we had extended ourselves more than at any time in our career to date. More than that, we had gone deeply into debt, even hocked our valuable film stock. Back in 1914, $40,000 was a lot of money. If our financial shoestring should break—

I wish French theater owner "Godspeed" as Carpentier-Dempsey fight films are loaded on plane.

THE PICTURE
IS
COMPLETED

Billie Burke, wife of Florenz Ziegfeld and an early Aitken star, in photo taken at Inceville, a Triangle Studio.

How Griffith managed to produce the twelve reel *Birth of a Nation* within a year is still a film industry feat which many cannot understand, especially since it was done on a part time basis. Henry Walthall, Lillian Gish, Mae Marsh and Raoul Walsh told me they recalled how an inspired, dynamic Griffith drove himself and his players at a terrific pace day after day. He would not rest until the picture was completed. He became irritable when there were delays.

The second point that amazed the film world was the liberal attitude of the Majestic Film Company's board of directors in allowing the Griffith-Aitken syndicate to use their facilities at cost, plus ten percent, for the filming of a picture in which they had no proprietary right. Probably no other film company of that time would have countenanced such an arrangement.

But the reason they did was always clear to Harry and me. Harry had created Majestic Film Company and was its president. The board recognized him as an organizational and promotional genius who had built the company into a top-rank producing unit. Majestic, at the time of the filming of the *Birth of a Nation,* was undoubtedly larger and its products better known than the Zukor and Laemmle interests. The board had faith in Harry, and while it would not help finance the *Birth* picture, felt that it would be therapeutic for Harry and Griffith to get this epic virus out of their blood; then they might be more content to stick with standard, shorter Majestic productions.

Too, the Majestic board was fully aware that Griffith had a contract with them which paid him only $300 per week, much less than he could get elsewhere. But the contract had the special clause which Griffith loved, and it was this clause that was the principal factor in keeping Griffith from jumping to Adolph Zukor. The Majestic board knew that this was the only sort of contract which could keep Griffith satisfied. Kahn and Livingston, and most of the other Majestic board members, also sat on the board of our Reliance Company which we had earlier bought from New York Motion Picture Corporation. They also sat on the Mutual Film Corporation board. This latter firm Harry and I had organized with the help of J. R. Freuler, a friend from Milwaukee. Freuler also owned the American Film Company of Chicago, which was producing some short pictures.

Harry was president of Reliance and Mutual, too. We distributed those pictures, along with the output of the Fine Arts, Sennett and Ince studios. Many of these films were known as Mutual Master Pictures and were widely advertised.

Mutual was the first American film company to buy full page advertisements in the *Saturday Evening Post.* The ads featured Mutual movies and the directors who made them.

H. B. Warner and Dorothy Dalton in **The Raiders.**

HB Warner in The Raiders © Triangle P

Harry also inspired the creation of a Mutual Girl trademark and used a slogan, "Mutual Movies Make Time Fly," which was placed beneath the insignia of a clock with the hour hand turning rapidly.

Administering the affairs of these companies, the big Mutual distribution organization and our own film exchanges, both in the United States and abroad, plus trying to finance such ventures, gave Harry and me many worries in those hectic days. And, of course, Griffith's spending splurge on the experimental twelve reel *Birth of a Nation* was one of them.

"I am disturbed," Harry wrote me in London in October 1914. "I have been to Hollywood again and just can't talk sense to Griffith. *The Clansman,* as they have decided to name the picture, will be a thrilling movie judging from the rushes I have seen. It may do well, but not as well perhaps as Griffith believes. He is constantly expanding battle and other scenes and adding expensive costuming.

"I understand that he made 150,000 feet of negatives, then cut yardage to 30,000 ft. and then to 12,000 ft. with the help of Raoul Walsh and Joseph Hennaberry. All that film cost a lot of money. Griffith and I had some stormy sessions on cost, similar to those when you and I were here earlier. Griffith isn't used to being stood up to, and I'm afraid we are not as close as we once were."

Harry said he had reluctantly agreed to raise another $19,000 for Griffith as a final concession to maintain harmony. That brought the total Aitken investment in the picture to $59,000. And that was $19,000 more than the amount Griffith had originally asked for and which we had promised.

Whereas formerly, Harry wrote, we had hocked almost all our film holdings to provide Griffith with $40,000 for the picture, we had now—with an additional $19,000 commitment to friends—almost hocked our souls, too.

And what had Griffith risked financially as of this date? Nothing!

If the *Birth* failed, Harry and I would owe $59,000 to a lot of creditors. And if we couldn't pay up—

"I got the extra $19,000," Harry wrote, "but we are liable for it. When I sent Griffith a credit memo I told him it would be the last he would get from us for his *Clansman* picture—that he should finish the film and put it on the market."

Harry also wrote that he had hired a J. C. Epping, an accountant, through Majestic Film Company, to take up residence on the Coast and to supervise the issuing of moneys to Ince, Sennett and Griffith.

"Perhaps it's too late," Harry wrote, "but at least from now on we have an agent on the scene whose job it is to make our money stretch as far as possible."

43

At this time, too, we had many well-known authors writing scripts for our companies. Irvin Cobb, Richard Harding Davis, Booth Tarkington and others were coming to parties at our New York apartment and some were selling stories to us for screen adaptations. Later, Mary Roberts Rinehart began selling us stories. Not only did she sell us scripts, but also, when we were on the West Coast, often played poker with us at the Beverly Hills Hotel—and usually beat us badly.

The Aitkens, in 1914, if I may say so, were regarded as successful movie entrepreneurs. We lacked only one thing—a stabilizer known as money. I knew the risk we were taking in expanding such a movie empire without financing, and Harry knew too. But there was so much to gain if we succeeded.

Thinking of all this, I decided it was time for me to take a trip back to the States. The foreign exchanges were doing all right, but sometimes movie audiences were small in the theaters we served, because of blackouts, especially in London. Even though embroiled in a war, the British and French sought constant film entertainment as a temporary escape from war tensions. Theaters in neutral countries, too, were eager to get more American films.

I left a capable colleague, Thomas E. Davies, in charge of the London office and sailed for the States. When I got to our New York office the following fortnight, Harry seemed quite perturbed.

"I understand Griffith is now selling stock in *The Clansman* picture," he said. "And I don't like that, for it complicates ownership, makes the picture more costly and increases the risk of the investment. I have one of his stock forms here, which a friend on the West Coast sent to me. In this proposal, Griffith mentions that the Aitkens have invested fifty-five thousand dollars to date in *his* picture. He's four thousand off. We've put in fifty-nine thousand dollars and Majestic money transfer credits will show it. I wrote Griffith

That was strong language for Harry. I knew that discussion between Griffith and him must have been very heated. Usually they could settle their differences. Griffith would boil when he learned he not only had to ask Epping for every $1,000 he wanted to spend, but also had to explain why.

I was worried. Harry and I had so much of our personal fortunes invested in Griffith's epic, that if the partners in the special picture became estranged, our movie empire might be weakened seriously.

Our movie companies and film exchanges were growing rapidly and the future looked promising. We were getting all the important stars who were anxious to work for Griffith, Sennett, and Ince. I wanted nothing to interfere with this growth of influence.

this was our picture—yours and mine—as far as financing was concerned, and that we didn't want him to sell more stock than the amount we had invested. We want controlling interest."

Harry also told me that Majestic's special representative said Griffith had drawn all of the $59,000 to date and was furious that Harry had refused to raise more. Epping also said that Griffith was tramping the streets of Los Angeles trying to sell additional stock.

One big investor Griffith secured, we learned, was J. R. Clune, a Los Angeles theater owner. Griffith had induced Clune to come to the Fine Arts studio to watch a Klan scene being filmed.

As Clune watched, a large group of gray-clad Confederates marched up the street while a band played *Dixie*. Clune, who was proud of his theater orchestra, exclaimed, "That would be a wonderful scene to show in my theater! And how my orchestra would play Dixie!"

So he told Griffith he would invest $5,000 to help him complete the epic, if Griffith would open the movie in his Los Angeles theater. Griffith agreed.

Because we allowed Griffith to solicit additional funds to finance his *Clansman* picture, we got into quite a financial tangle some months later.

William S. Hart, famous Aitken star, sells Liberty Bonds during World War I. He is shown standing in automobile across the street from Royal Theater, Brooklyn, where one of his pictures was playing.

THE BIRTH

AT

LOS ANGELES

Birth of a Nation battle scene showing Union Charge during Battle of Petersburg.

Finally, on February 8, 1915, Griffith was ready to unveil his epic *Clansman* at Clune's Auditorium Theater in Los Angeles. As principal investors, Harry and I came out from New York to attend. Griffith purposely avoided us, and we were not too anxious to talk to him until we had seen the complete motion picture. We wanted to decide without his sales talk if our $59,000 investment was safe, and if the picture was good enough to show promise of making sufficient profit to pay back all the investors. The rumor that a total of $110,000 had now been spent in making and promoting the picture was a newsy topic of conversation in the film world.

Clune's theater was filled as the *Clansman* picture began to unreel. Clune's orchestra was ready. They played sentimental music during the tender love scenes between Henry Walthall and Lillian Gish, and they played martial music when the call to colors came. This military music swelled to swift crescendo when the cannons roared, as bullets tore battle flags to shreds, and soldiers fell to their death.

Then later in the film when Confederate soldiers marched up the street of a Southern town, flying the Rebel flag, Clune's orchestra spiritedly struck up *Dixie*. They played it so enthusiastically I felt like getting up to cheer and wave my hat.

Harry gripped the arms of his seat. "It's a wonderful picture, Roy," he whispered. "I've got to hand it to D. W. even if he spent all that money. Perhaps this picture will surprise many people—even us."

Thomas Dixon sat near us. His breath came rapidly as the stirring war scenes swept across the screen. "The picture is better than the the *Clansman* book!" he exclaimed. "And it needs a better title. This picture is—like the birth of a nation. That's it—the *Birth of a Nation*!"

Thus the photoplay got its remarkable title —one with sales appeal.

We met an exuberant, flushed Griffith as we pushed through the noisy crowd in the lobby. The lean lines in Griffith's face were gone. He was smiling. "How did you like it, Harry?" he asked triumphantly.

"Marvelous," Harry said warmly. "You've produced a great picture, D. W. Now we are ready to show it in New York."

We spent two days in Los Angeles with Griffith and Dixon. We wanted to know who the other stockholders were and how much they had actually invested in the picture. At lunch at the Alexandria Hotel, Harry scribbled the names and the amounts of stock on the back of an envelope as Griffith dictated.

The total came to $110,000—as rumor had previously announced. Of that amount, the Aitkens had invested $59,000, or controlling interest. Some of this money had not been used, Griffith pointed out. But it would soon be needed, he added, for promotion of the *Birth* in New York.

Griffith's first wife in her book *When Movies Were Young* (1925) says that the

Aitkens financed the *Birth* to the amount of $60,000 and that the remaining $55,000 was in additional costs. I mention this now, because so many rumors have circulated claiming that Griffith owned the picture and had financed it.

The truth of the matter was that financially Griffith had no monetary interest in the *Birth*. When Harry and Griffith set out on their own to finance the *Birth* after Majestic refused to put up the money, the special picture clause in the Majestic contract did not apply to the *Birth*. So far as I know, Harry and Griffith merely had a verbal agreement on sharing the *Birth's* profits, but when the chips were down the partner who had invested the most money won out. Especially so, when the other partner, Griffith, had no money invested.

But at that Alexandria Hotel luncheon table an agreement was worked out. Dixon, of course, had a prior agreement of twenty-five percent royalty on the net profits. Harry now agreed to give Griffith a thirty-seven and a half percent profit after Dixon's royalty had been paid. Then—on what profit remained —the rest of the stockholders were to be paid. This, I thought, was a very fair arrangement.

"I want to tell you, Harry," said Griffith somberly, "that I have organized the D. W. Griffith Corporation to handle my interests and those of my investors in any special pictures I make with you or entirely on my own. I have pledged the additional *Birth* investors I'd see that they got their money back at a profit."

This was news to Harry and me. We were surprised to learn that Griffith had organized his own production company, but saw nothing wrong in that. We thought, however, that he should have informed us earlier.

The excitement all of us felt about the *Birth of a Nation* and the promise of its future, caused us to turn our minds toward the New York opening. If the picture got as stirring a reception there as it had in Los Angeles, then we could look forward to a big run. And that was what we needed.

"We'll get the Liberty Theater," Harry said enthusiastically, "and we'll have an invitational matinee. Special guests, movie critics, and other influential people. And we'll have theme music. I like what Clune did here. The music adds to the picture."

John R. Freuler, our partner in film exchange and Mutual Film Corp.

"I do, too," Dixon said. "The music deepens the mood. How much admission shall we charge in New York?"

"Perhaps a dollar a ticket," suggested Griffith.

Harry looked up quickly. "A dollar! For such an expensive picture? How will we ever get our money back? I say two dollars per ticket."

Griffith gasped. "It's too much, Harry. Movie admissions in New York are ten and twenty-five cents."

"This is not an ordinary movie," Harry insisted.

"I know it," said Griffith proudly.

"Then let's get what it's worth—two dollars. Okay, Roy?"

I nodded.

Harry won the argument. Mrs. Griffith in her book also gives Harry credit for establishing the $2.00 price. She says Griffith and Dixon argued with him for a long time, but that Harry finally won. In a magazine interview some years later, Griffith claimed that the $2.00 price was his idea—but he was always quick to claim credits whenever he could.

Harry and I went back to New York the following day and began to make arrangements for the Liberty Theater showing. Griffith and Dixon were to follow in a few days. Dixon was happy about the success of the *Birth of a Nation*. No doubt he could clearly see that if the picture grossed well, his twenty-five percent royalty would net him much more than the $25,000 cash he had originally wanted as an outright sale of the photoplay rights. Griffith was happy too. He was acclaimed a genius and his epic a masterpiece. Now that recognition and fortune beckoned, Griffith's sense of his greatness deepened and,

Raoul Walsh as a bit player in early Aitken
picture. He played part of John Wilkes Booth
in **Birth of a Nation**.

definitely, he became more autocratic. Many
people noticed the change in the great director.

A couple of days later at our New York
office, Harry told me, "Our lawyer has just
informed me that Griffith has copyrighted the
picture in the name of the D. W. Griffith
Corporation." He looked a little worried.

"Oh?"

Harry nodded. "On the Coast, Griffith and
I had talked about a new company to handle
the *Birth*, but nothing definite was decided.
Griffith was quick to protect his interest by
copyrighting the *Birth*. Actually he owns nothing of it, yet—he has no money invested. So
I'll bet he now asks to buy some stock in
addition to the royalty agreement."

This surmise later proved correct, but we
were too busy that day making plans for the
premiere showing of the *Birth* in New York
to worry about Griffith's motives. Harry felt
that since we were the majority investors,
we could dictate the final settlement terms.

A further obstacle came up. Mutual Film
Corporation expected to get the distribution
rights to the *Birth* picture. They asked Harry
and me to give them a preview of the picture
at a board meeting, so they could appraise it.

We did this one afternoon at an office at 60
Wall Street, with the full Mutual board in attendance. "An exciting picture," J. R. Freuler
said enthusiastically.

Felix Kahn and Crawford Livingston merely
shrugged. They thought the picture no better
than the many cheaper standard four reelers
that Majestic and Reliance companies were
turning out for Mutual distribution. Freuler,
a pretty shrewd film man, however, said he
wanted the *Birth* on the Mutual list.

On the way back to our Majestic office,
Harry looked worried. "Many of the investors
Griffith sold in California don't want to turn
over the picture to Mutual to distribute. They
want a separate distributing company. Perhaps they are right."

I shrugged. "If you help form another distribution company, can you hold your post as
Mutual president?"

"I don't know. Freuler would like to be
president of Mutual and I can't blame him
for being so ambitious. Hutchinson, his American Film Company manager, is very bitter
toward us because I wouldn't let Mutual distribute a couple of risqué pictures he'd made.
But I think the public expects Mutual to distribute clean pictures. So long as I am with
Mutual we won't need to be ashamed of films
we rent to theaters."

Now that I look back, some forty-nine years
later, I believe this was the first instance of
censorship of films. Everyone who knew
Harry and his religious background knew that
he championed clean pictures and that he
often fought for this policy.

"We've got another problem," Harry said.
"Some of the friends we borrowed money
from to help finance the *Birth* need their
money. Knowing they couldn't get it from us
at this time, they sold the notes we gave them."

"To whom?"

Harry grimaced. "To persons who heard
the news out of Los Angeles—that the *Birth
of a Nation* was an outstanding motion picture
—Freuler and certain other directors on the
Mutual board. They want to make sure they
get in on a good thing."

"And if you help organize a separate company to distribute the *Birth?*"

Harry shrugged. "I suppose they'll ask me
to buy their stock immediately—try to em-
barrass us. They know we're short on personal cash."

I sighed. "Once in a while I wish I had stayed
in Wisconsin, Harry. Every week we run into
some new trouble in this movie business."

"Why not?" grinned Harry. "The stakes are
big. Everyone plays for himself. And if you
get hurt no one will bind your wounds. You
do it alone, or else—"

Two days later Harry helped in the formation of the Epoch Producing Corporation
whose sole purpose was to distribute the

Marble Arch
Pavilion,
London,
England

Birth of a Nation motion picture. And Harry became the first president of Epoch.

Before the deal went through, however, Griffith showed his hand. He wanted not only to keep his royalty agreement, but he also wanted the opportunity to purchase some $5,000 worth of stock—a hundred eighty shares.

A number of stockholders agreed to give up a share here and there—so did we—and that is how Griffith finally got his stock. Harry and I still retained controlling interest in Epoch, based on our investment. Griffith claimed a number of times that he owned the *Birth of a Nation,* that it was his picture. From an artistic and production viewpoint it *was* his picture. I will not deny that. But Epoch records show that from the date of organization the Aitkens owned controlling interest.

In return for the right to buy stock in Epoch, Griffith agreed to assign the D. W. Griffith Corporation copyright of the *Birth of a Nation* to Epoch. This is what should have been done in the first place, but events had moved so fast after the completion of the movie in California and its Los Angeles showing that the Epoch Company idea was not born until a few weeks before the picture was ready for its first New York showing.

I could never get Harry to tell me whether Griffith intended to keep the *Birth of a Nation* copyright for the D. W. Griffith Corporation, or whether he wanted to use it only as a bargaining ace. But the facts showed Griffith acted very rapidly in his own behalf by copyrighting the epic as soon as it was completed. If he had other intentions, they were known only to himself.

Now as we readied the *Birth* for its New York premiere, things began to happen at Mutual. Freuler and his associates, angry because Harry had formed Epoch and Mutual would not get distribution of the *Birth of a Nation,* began to work behind the scenes.

There was a reshuffling of forces at Mutual, and Harry was finally voted out as president, and Freuler was elected in his place. Then the Mutual directors who had bought *Birth* stock demanded that Harry pay up the notes they held. Luckily, Harry was able to get new loans from others to do this.

The Majestic Film Company and Reliance Film Company, however, still kept Harry as president, for many of the directors in those film producing companies felt that Harry's imaginative guidance was needed there. Mutual, of course, still said it would distribute Majestic and Reliance pictures, but it was Freuler who held the guiding reins on distribution, not Harry.

This was a split which would soon have other far-reaching effects.

LIBERTY THEATER

OPENING

Bobby Harron (holding bill) played the part of
Tod Stoneman in **Birth of a Nation**.

While Griffith was in New York with us preparing to show the *Birth of a Nation,* his California staff of six sub-directors continued to produce standard two to four reel pictures at our Majestic Fine Arts studio. This left Griffith free to spend several weeks working out the details for the grand opening of his epic picture. Majestic Film Company had offices at 60 Wall Street and Griffith was assigned a separate room with stenographer. Here he concentrated on the many details which accompany the premiere of a motion picture. And since the *Birth* would make history as being the first picture to be shown in an important theater and at a $2.00 admission price, Griffith had to do some pioneer promoting.

I think these weeks were some of the most exciting of my life. All of us connected with the *Birth* picture felt that we were on the brink of great developments in our industry, and it was wonderful to be a part of it.

I got to know Griffith well during this period. Harry assigned me to help him in whatever way I could. Griffith loved to drive around New York, and so I frequently lent him one of our foreign cars and our Wisconsin chauffeur, Matt Hosely. Once in a while Griffith took the Bollee, or the Renault, and drove it himself—to relax from the pressure of work, he said.

Griffith and I often dined downtown at the Old Waldorf, or at the Algonquin Hotel, which was a favorite gathering place for producers and actors. Operated by Frank Case, a patron of the arts, the Algonquin dining room used many tablecloths. The Aitkens, Griffith, and many others got into the habit of outlining theatrical promotion campaigns on the white tablecloths. But Case didn't mind.

Sometimes we dined at our West Fifty-seventh Street apartment with Harry and Dixon. Occasionally, Griffith and I brought a couple of models or actresses along to dinner. I had a new player piano at the apartment, and Griffith loved to dance. The piano was so set up that when the apartment door opened, the player piano began to pour forth music. This was in the days when player pianos were just coming on the market. This novelty feature always surprised and entertained the guests.

It was at one of the apartment dinners that I heard Harry and Griffith discuss over dessert a motion picture Griffith had made while the *Birth* was in production. It was a picture called *The Mother and the Law,* and was produced as a Griffith-Aitken film. It featured Robert Harron and Mae Marsh, among others. Griffith said he was intrigued with the idea of the picture and that someday he hoped to lengthen it with more episodes, depending on the reaction of the public to the shorter film. *The Mother and the Law* was later made into the famous *Intolerance* by Griffith. Harry told me several times that almost $200,000 of Aitken money was invested in it, and that we never did get our investment back. I don't know, because in those topsy-turvy days, we raced to keep pace with current duties, and I left financial matters mostly to Harry. I was content to have stock in all of the companies and to be a part of this exciting business.

The selection of theme music for the *Birth of a Nation* premiere obsessed Griffith. He had noticed how the audience reacted to keyed music at the Los Angeles showing. He interviewed many musicians in New York and worked with a number of them selecting suitable music and synchronizing it to the action of the picture. Thus the *Birth* music consisted of excerpts from operatic numbers and also folk tunes such as *In The Gloaming*, and *Home Sweet Home*.

Once he had selected his orchestra, Griffith worked tirelessly with the musicians. He ran the film time and again, scheduling the music and tempo he wanted for special scenes. I spent many hours in the Liberty Theater watching Griffith. He was a tireless enthusiast.

One scene always brought tears to my eyes, and it still does. It is the sequence where Henry Walthall, the Little Confederate Colonel, comes limping home after the war, wondering if the house he knew as home still stands.

The street is deserted and so is the yard of his home. Walthall limps wearily up the porch steps and knocks. For a moment, no answer. Then the door slowly opens. A pair of thin arms reach out and draw Walthall lovingly inside. While the scene is shown, the orchestra plays *Home Sweet Home*. In fact, this scene is one of the most touching in the entire picture.

It has often been said that music was synchronized to film action for the first time with the showing of the *Birth*, and a yellowed sheet in my files lists the orchestra parts for the picture.

News of the elaborate preparations for the showing of the *Birth* soon trickled up and down Broadway, of course. The legitimate stage crowd was frankly contemptuous. Owners and actors were irked that a motion picture dared to compete on Broadway and at the same price as a stage play. Many stage managers predicted we would soon fail, if we stuck to the ridiculous price of $2.00 per person to "see a flicker."

This attitude reflected quite accurately the general position of the motion picture in 1915. The working and lower middle classes had quickly accepted the movie as a popular form of entertainment and within their price ranges. These people did not care whether the flickers had stature as art. They liked the action, suspense, and comedy in the films and continued to pay their nickels and dimes for screen thrills. But many sophisticated people disdained the current movies and spoke disparagingly of them. "Just a passing fad," many said.

This was also the attitude of many of the movie production personnel and some of the players. "We're all in a magic fairyland," petite Mabel Normand told me. "No one knows when the bubble will burst, so let's have a good time while it lasts."

Such a lack of confidence in the new industry was not shared by Harry and me, although Griffith has been said to have harbored a secret dislike of the medium until the success of the *Birth of a Nation*. Harry and I and a few others associated with us, however, were real movie fans. We felt that motion pictures would grow in influence and some day could compete artistically with top stage productions.

Finally the plans for showing the *Birth* at the Liberty Theater took shape. We decided to hold a free invitational matinee on February 28th, 1915, with the formal opening on March 3rd at the $2.00 admission price. A matinee held a week or so prior to the grand opening would build suspense and attendance for a later run, we decided.

Prior to the matinee showing, Harry and Thomas Dixon took the *Birth* to Washington, D. C., and showed it to President Wilson and his family.

Before Harry and Dixon could leave Washington, they received an invitation to show the film privately to the Justices of the Supreme Court and other officials. The group gathered at the National Press Club for the viewing, and the Justices were enthusiastic about the picture. This news, of course, helped to build interest in the picture in New York.

A Schubert publicity man named Theodore Mitchell was urged by Harry to see a private preview of the *Birth* in New York. Mitchell, a devoted stage fan, was reluctant to take the time to see the *Birth*, but as a result of Harry's persistence, he finally consented. When the show ended, Mitchell's face was flushed. "I want to handle publicity for that picture!" he said. "It's great!"

Mitchell brought another Schubert publicity man, J. R. McCarthy, to meet Harry.

Within a matter of hours, the two men had signed a contract with Harry to handle publicity and promotion for the *Birth*. These men proved to be trail blazers for motion picture publicity. One of their best ideas was to hire white-robed horsemen to gallop down the streets of a city to the theater where the *Birth* was showing. This was the first of a number of picture exploitation stunts which mushroomed all over the nation. Many of the promotional devices used by movie theaters today are patterned after the tactics employed by Mitchell and McCarthy.

"Well, Roy," Harry said wearily as we went to bed at 3 a.m. the night before the invitational matinee, "within a matter of fifteen hours we will know what the hard-boiled New York reaction is to our costly *Birth of a Nation*. If it is good, then the picture should have a long run, and we can get some money to pay off many of our obligations. If it doesn't do well?" He hesitated.

"Let's not think about that." I said, yawning. "Let's go to sleep."

But I did not fall asleep immediately. I couldn't help thinking how much this picture meant to Harry and me. Of all the movies we had financed, the *Birth* was the only one which conceivably could be a real money-maker. The other standard short movies by our various companies were forgotten less than a year after they were produced. So were the standard movies made by other producers. Pot boilers—most of us called them. They were made to satisfy the public's constantly increasing desire to see pictures, any pictures moving on a screen.

Picture of me in London in 1911.

Our matinee invitational list of society leaders, stage personalities, writers, artists, producers, and businessmen was carefully selected. Long before the show began, most of the seats in the theater were full and a large crowd waited out front. Through some mixup we had issued far too many invitations, and we were forced to put folding chairs in many of the aisles. This was an infraction of the law, but we had to take a chance.

Some people in the large audience listened to the orchestra playing classical music. Others watched the pretty uniformed girl ushers whom Griffith, ever the showman, had carefully selected and trained. This entertainment event, the people realized, would not be a movie presentation in a shabby run-down theater with meager furnishings; it would be exciting, colorful entertainment in a first-rate theater. The movies on Broadway—just think of it!

I stood in front of the theater, watching the surging crowd. Some were waving invitations; others just hoped to get in. I had only one press ticket left and just before the doors closed and the show was ready to start, I heard a loud voice. "Roy! Roy! Have you a seat for me?"

It was dark and handsome Tony Moreno, gasping for breath. "Yes, I have just one ticket left, Tony."

I gave him the folding chair I had tucked away for myself in the office, and then let him find his own viewing spot. Since I could find no seat for myself, I joined Harry, Griffith, and Dixon as they paced nervously up and down inside the lobby. Griffith's dark eyes gleamed. I think he was as thrilled as the rest of us were that the *Birth of a Nation* could attract such an important, overflow crowd. A playwright at heart, Griffith had always wanted to write a play good enough to be produced on Broadway. Well, Griffith was on Broadway now—not with a stage play, but with an exciting, promising new form of entertainment—a twelve reel motion picture. And he was the producer.

The lights in the theater darkened, and the orchestra swung into the theme music.

"Now we'll see this great epic," I heard a man say to a friend. "I'll bet the publicity is better than the picture."

The screen lighted and the forty piece orchestra keyed in. The picture moved into vision after the titling. Conversation faded quickly. There was silence as the picture moved faster across the screen and the explanatory sub-titles could be read. The audience could see the first slaves arriving in America and the ensuing abolition movement. Then came the Civil War period, showing Phil and Tod Stoneman of Pennsylvania visiting their school chums, the Cameron boys of South Carolina. The audience saw that Margaret Cameron (Miriam Cooper) was in love with Phil Stoneman, and Elsie Stoneman (Lillian Gish) was deeply in love with Colonel Ben Cameron (Henry Walthall).

One scene showed Henry Walthall making love to Lillian Gish while the orchestra played *In The Gloaming*. I heard a few women in the audience moan.

Later came the Civil War battle scenes. There were cheers and shouts at Griffith's improved movie techniques and his innovations —the panoramic battle scenes, the night photography, and the charge of the Klan horsemen directly over cameraman Billy Bitzer, who

Wallace Reed in Triangle production,
Old Heidelberg.

lay in a poorly protected hollow in the ground clicking off the scene.

At the intermission, there was silence for a few seconds. Then came cheers and prolonged applause. Many persons were so excited they did not know whether to sit down, stand up, go take a stroll into the lobby or go to get a strong drink. The *Birth of a Nation* had stirred the audience in a way that no other motion picture before had done. I think all of us knew we were seeing a picture which pointed new paths of fame for the flickers.

As the film showing resumed after the intermission, the crowd became quiet again. They were tense during the Reconstruction Era scenes, as they suffered with the hordes of war weary people without homes.

In Walthall's homecoming scene, I heard women groan compassionately as hands pulled the Little Colonel into a house battered by the poverty and violence of war. When the fleeing Mae Marsh leaped to her death from a high cliff to prevent being raped by a renegade, people grasped seat arms. And when the Ku Klux Klan came riding to the rescue, and the Klan bugle call rang out from the nearby orchestra pit, you could feel the chills go up your spine.

The final scene was gentle. It showed the remnants of the Stonemans and the Camerons

Promotion stills of members of cast
of **Birth of a Nation**.

The famous dance scene from *Birth of a Nation*.

united in a double wedding. The closing subtitle said, "The establishment of the South in its rightful place is the birth of a new nation."

The theater lights came on, and the applause was deafening. Minutes later it died down and then came the lower-pitched hubbub of excited conversation. People crowded around Griffith, Harry and Dixon. Society matrons were starry-eyed and sweetly effusive. Newspaper reporters writing drama columns had bewildered looks in their eyes, as if they could not yet comprehend how such a little-regarded medium as a motion picture had produced such effects. Promotors quickly tried to pull Harry, Griffith, and Dixon aside to whisper congratulations and urge propositions for exploitation of the picture, road showings, and purchase of stock in Epoch Producing Corporation.

Harry spotted me and came over to grasp my arm. "It's a hit, Roy!" he said excitedly. "Griffith and I are inviting some key people to the apartment tonight for a celebration. Phone Dunstan and Nellie to get ready. Then meet us at the Algonquin for something to eat."

I phoned Dunstan. "We're prepared," said our butler in his precise English. "Have you forgotten, Mr. Roy? Harry and you told me to lay in supplies, including beverages, just in case. I've even got quite a few of those salted nuts that Mr. Irvin Cobb likes."

Our celebration was not premature. If the *Birth* had pleased the elite and critics at the invitational matinee, we certainly could expect the resultant publicity would fill the $2.00 seats at the official premiere on March 3rd.

What a party that night at our seven room apartment! Fur coats, neckpieces, bowler hats, overcoats, scarves were piled high on beds in three bedrooms. Excited, bright-eyed people circulated through the big apartment, some drinking highballs, and some nibbling snacks. All talked eagerly about the *Birth of a Nation*. Felix Kahn and Crawford Livingston were there. Liquor glasses in hand, the bankers smiled and walked about a little self-consciously, perhaps wondering why so many people could get so excited about a motion picture.

Even the generally austere Thomas Dixon seemed at home as he glowed under the repeated praise for his books and the photoplay based on them. He nibbled tidbits, but drank no hard liquor.

Irvin Cobb stuck around the nut bowl, telling stories in his Kentucky drawl. Nina Wilcox Putnam was there, and so were Richard Harding Davis and many other authors who were selling us stories on which we could base movies. Messmore Kendall and his attractive wife were present. Kendall was later to build the Capitol Theater as a movie palace rather than as a vaudeville and stage theater, largely because of the success of the *Birth*.

The center of attention, of course, was David W. Griffith. Looking back, I don't think Harry and I were too envious of him. After all, the impression the *Birth of a Nation* made on the public was due to Griffith's artistry and direction. This was his moment of glory and he loved it. I began to notice from this time on, however, how much Griffith craved admiration and the public spotlight, and how much he missed it later in his life.

Long after the guests were gone, while Dunstan and Nellie wearily washed dishes in the kitchen, the phone rang. Harry, Griffith, Dixon and I were relaxing with final coffees and rejoicing only as successful partners in a great enterprise can.

Harry answered. A thick masculine voice said, "Hello, Aitken?. . . . This is Louis B. Mayer, Boston. . . . I've got a couple of theaters here. I've heard the story of the *Birth*'s successful matinee opening. How about selling me the New England distribution rights?"

A smile overspread Harry's cherubic face. He covered the transmitter with his hands and turned to us. "It's a Louis Mayer from Boston. He wants to buy distribution rights."

"Perhaps," chuckled Griffith. "For a big price. All of us need money."

"Mayer," said Harry, "how much will you offer?"

"Maybe fifty thousand, with a twenty-five thousand dollar down payment. And a fifty-fifty split after I get my investment back."

"Come to New York as soon as you can," Harry invited, "and we'll talk to you about the deal. But hurry—you'll have competitors. Our two dollar grand opening will be next week and if it's a sellout, our distribution prices may go up."

That was how we got to know Louis B. Mayer. Later, Mayer contracted for the New England distribution rights for $50,000 and he made more than a half million dollars on the deal. With this profit he moved to Hollywood and eventually became head of MGM.

Four years after the *Birth of a Nation* was produced, Mayer bought our famous Culver City studio in California. This was the studio we had erected for Thomas Ince and his popular Western and mystery productions. The Aitkens at this time were moving fast—but Mayer moved faster. It was from the Culver City studio that Mayer directed a tremendous expansion of MGM operations, at a personal salary of one million dollars a year.

55

CENSORSHIP

AND BOYCOTT

Cover of pamphlet
protesting showing of film.

WHY

WE FIGHT THE

"BIRTH OF A NATION"

AN OPEN LETTER TO PUBLIC SENTIMENT

Resolution Adopted March 7th by City Commissioners

In view of the fact that the film play known as the "Birth of a Nation," is creating strenuous objection to its presentation by the citizens of Dayton, Ohio, and in view of the fact that it is considered and recognized as a hatred breeding film, as opposed to amicable relations between the white and colored citizenship, be it resolved,

That out of deference to the well-being of all citizens, the Commissioners of Dayton, Ohio, condemn the presentation of the "Birth of a 'Nation film at this time, and lend their influence, both severally and collectively, in an effort to prohibit its exhibitions.

All of us who were associated with the *Birth of a Nation* were dazed with the success the picture achieved at the Liberty Theater. Newspapers carried enthusiastic articles concerning the film's dramatic and artistic qualities. One reporter wrote that the *Birth* definitely showed the way to epic stories on the screen. Another asserted that the film revealed the possibilities of the art of the movies for the first time.

Actually, the interest aroused in the movies by the *Birth of a Nation* is credited by a number of newspaper men as responsible for the establishment of regular motion picture reviews by New York and other news mediums.

Many prominent people made statements to the press about the picture. One was Charles Frohman, renowned stage producer, who saw the *Birth of a Nation* several times. "I have lived to see what I have never expected would happen in my lifetime," he said. "A movie at two dollars a ticket!"

De Wolfe Hopper, who was on the New York stage, told newsmen he was converted to the motion picture idea by viewing the *Birth of a Nation*. "I saw a wonderful thing," he said. "I saw an audience held spellbound as I have rarely seen an audience held in the theater. I saw their excitement, saw their tears. The picture itself, with its many infinitely dramatic touches—strokes of genius—struck me as something big, something new, something important. I came out dazed."

Hopper later signed with us to make a series of motion pictures.

But there was also considerable criticism of the *Birth of a Nation* because of its racial implications. The National Association for the Advancement of Colored People vigorously protested against its showing. President Charles Eliot of Harvard charged the picture with perverting white ideals. Jane Adams spoke against it.

Oswald Garrison Villard, militant editor of the *Nation,* said the picture was a deliberate attempt to humiliate ten million American citizens and portray them as nothing but beasts. Francis Hackett in the *New Republic* called Thomas Dixon a yellow clergyman, and Booker T. Washington wrote indignant letters to many newspapers attacking the picture. Albert Bigelow Paine, noted journalist, wrote, "The picture is within the facts, but hardly within the proprieties."

Harry had shown the *Birth of a Nation* to the National Board of Censorship in New York, about two weeks after the Los Angeles opening, and got a recommendation from that body. The board was unofficial, but its opinion was accepted almost everywhere in the United States at the time. In fact, the board's report on the film stated that the film's educational value was excellent, the artistic value excellent, and its moral effect good. Further comment was, "educationally and artistically this should prove a great step forward in motion picture production."

Then, two days before the *Birth* opened in New York, the National Association for the Advancement of Colored People obtained a re-hearing, and the picture was shown to their delegates and the National Board of Censorship. Some of the colored people hissed the picture. After the hearing, the National Board of Censorship revoked its approval of the picture.

The NAACP then claimed the picture would cause race riots. They arranged for a hearing before Chief Justice William McAdoo of the Court of General Sessions in New York. After consideration, Justice McAdoo determined that there was not sufficient cause for racial apprehension and refused an application for an injunction.

Undeterred, the NAACP then went to John Purroy Mitchell, Mayor of the City of New York, for the purpose of having the commissioner of licenses revoke the license of the Liberty Theater where the *Birth* was showing. But this move failed, and the *Birth* continued to play. But the NAACP was never to relax its efforts to keep the *Birth of a Nation* off the movie screens of the United States. They are still protesting the showing of the picture today.

"I hope this minority opposition won't keep people from seeing the picture, Harry," I said to him at lunch one day.

Harry smiled. "It won't, Roy. The public won't stay home now. They will want to judge for themselves whether or not the picture will incite to riot. This is a free country. The people want to make their own decisions on which pictures they wish to see."

And Harry was right. Afternoon and evening, the Liberty theater was filled to overflowing. The press, many clergymen and businessmen praised the picture. And, as it turned out, the *Birth of a Nation* was destined to run continuously at the Liberty for forty-eight weeks.

Harry E. Aitken in his office in 1912
when he was President of Mutual Film Corp.

Epoch Producing Corporation, as owner and distributor of the picture, was now faced with an important decision. Practically all the stockholders needed money, or wanted some quick cash return on investments. Harry and I especially needed money, for we had borrowed most of the $59,000 we had invested in the picture and our creditors were asking for payment. Epoch had the choice of trying to organize road shows for the *Birth* picture, or of accepting some of the large cash offers for state distribution rights.

Ambitious and shrewd promotors were contacting us daily. Louis B. Mayer haunted our offices, offering to pay $50,000 ($25,000 down payment) with a fifty-fifty split on net profits after he got his original payment back. Mayer's partner was Daniel Stoneham, a wealthy Bostonian.

Harry Sherman of Minneapolis offered $100,000 cash for the rights to sixteen western states, plus a fifty-fifty split on net profits. J. R. Clune and David Griffith offered a large sum for state rights in California. Al Woods, New York theatrical producer, came up with a $250,000 offer for world's rights and a fifty-fifty split on net profits.

As I sat at a tense Epoch meeting in mid-March, I could hardly believe that such huge offers were being made to us, for we had had to work hard for many years to coax money into our coffers. Was the tide about to turn, I wondered, even though the specter of censorship and boycotting loomed large?

Harry was president of Epoch. "We need more capital if we are to organize road companies and show the *Birth* in selected cities," he told the board. "If we sell a few state distribution rights, we can use some of that cash to finance a number of our road shows in cities outside the franchised areas. On the other hand, if we want to cover the entire United States with our road shows—and sell no state rights—we'll have to get a huge sum of money somewhere to finance the project."

"I think we'd better take the best offers on state rights," said A. J. Banzhaf, a lawyer-director, "and then get the rest of the money from our selected road shows. After all, this picture may not pull forever. Attendance could taper off quickly. Let's get all the cash we can now."

The Epoch board finally voted to sell New England rights to Mayer and Stoneham for $50,000, but held out Boston for our own road show. Also accepted was the bid of Harry Sherman for $100,000 for sixteen western states. Clune and Griffith got California, but the board turned down Al Wood's bid of $250,000 for world's rights.

Closeup of Confederate Army at Petersburg,
with Henry Walthall as commander of unit.

These sums were big money back in 1915 when the purchasing power of a dollar was many times greater than what it is today. With state rights money in our hands—over $200,000—we were able to proceed immediately to finance and outfit elaborate road shows. Within a few months we had twenty such shows traveling the nation in cities not in franchised areas. Each road show was complete with manager, publicity chief, and a twenty to forty piece orchestra.

I remember that I was delegated by the board to accompany Harry Sherman to our Wall Street bank one day, so he could deposit his $100,000 check to our account.

I recall that Sherman, destined to become a movie mogul in a few years, was quite proud as he handed his check to our banker. "I'll bet you don't see many checks this big," Sherman said.

The banker smiled, walked to one of the cages and came back with a check. He showed it to Sherman. It was for a million dollars!

I told my brother of this incident that night in our apartment after the rush of visitors had left. "Well, Sherman may have been a little taken back at the sight of that big check," Harry said, "but a hundred thousand dollars is still a lot of money. Sherman's no fool. He knows what he's doing. He figures he can make a lot of money on the *Birth of a Nation.*"

Again Harry was right. Sherman made his million plus, then went to California as a producer and eventually launched William Boyd into the popular Hopalong Cassidy series that captivated so many American youngsters.

Actually, had Harry and I known what a long-time money maker the *Birth of a Nation* was destined to be—over $50,000,000 gross from 1915 through 1960—I think we would have been more hesitant about selling state distribution rights. Had we held onto those rights and exploited the *Birth* ourselves, we would have made the extra millions which state rights promoters and theater owners got from the *Birth* showings in their choice territories.

But most of Epoch's stockholders were tired of the tension of shoestring financing, and all of us yearned to pay debts and reward ourselves with a few luxuries which had long been denied us. We were gamblers, but this was our conservative moment, I suppose.

I peer into 1900 model "Mutoscope," penny arcade moving picture device, while Thurman Fox (left) and Paul Vanderbilt (right) watch.

I think it is important to remember that our road shows of the *Birth of a Nation* played at the best theaters throughout the areas we covered, and that the price was still $2.00 for top tickets. The smaller movie theaters could not accommodate large audiences, and the Epoch board sternly insisted, too, that the *Birth* play in the largest and finest theaters. I think these road shows did much to convince many men with money that it could be a profitable venture for them to erect large theaters for the showing of outstanding motion pictures.

"Money!" Harry chuckled one night at dinner in our New York apartment. "At last we've got it, Roy. It is pouring in from every direction. We're paying many of our debts and we're living better. The *Birth* is a bigger success than any of us ever dreamed. Next week, less than two months after the Liberty opening, Epoch will declare its first dividend."

Dividends! Between June 15, 1915, and August 2, 1916, Epoch stockholders received forty-one dividends ranging from five to twenty-five percent! No wonder people began besieging Epoch stockholders to try to buy in on the distribution company at almost any price. But no one was selling.

By mid-1916, the *Birth* had shown to more than a million people in New York alone. The trend was the same all over the nation. The *Birth* attendance records were amazing. Even the stage crowd was impressed.

59

DEFENSE

OF THE PICTURE

Booth leaving theater box after shooting Lincoln, as portrayed in scene from **Birth of a Nation**.

But censorship and boycott troubles were increasing, too. Even as the *Birth* profits rolled in, the NAACP was increasingly active in Boston and elsewhere. The organization claimed that the *Birth* was inciting race riots, and Boston newspapers were filled with articles about NAACP protests.

The furor disturbed Harry and me as well as many other Epoch officers. Many of us felt that Griffith had dealt as fairly with the Negro question as was possible within the facts. He had balanced the Negro renegade participation in Reconstruction affairs with the actions of the faithful, lovable plantation Negro. He clearly revealed that extreme Negro reactions were instigated by white carpetbaggers. He followed history texts closely on this.

Anyone who has read Thomas Dixon's *Clansman* knows that Griffith's script treats the Negro much more sympathetically than did Dixon's novel. And Epoch, over the years, did eliminate scenes and titles in the *Birth of a Nation* upon occasion where certain minority groups insisted. But to remove the entire picture from the screen—that was something else.

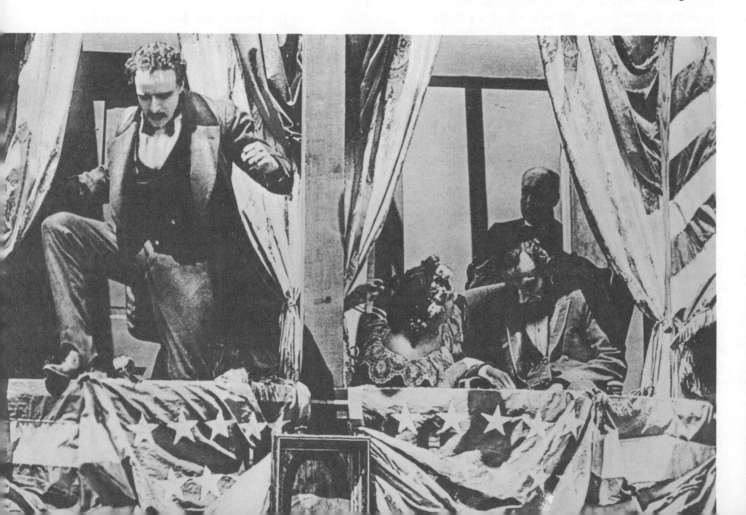

Henry Walthall as commander of
Confederate forces at Battle of Petersburg.

"Griffith is quite upset about this Boston situation," Harry told me one day. "In fact, he's going up there for two days and will speak at the Tremont Theater before each show in defense of the picture. And he told me he will travel anywhere to speak for the *Birth of a Nation*. He feels strongly that a motion picture is entitled to the same freedom of expression as is the press, and he will fight for it."

While the NAACP and other minority groups rolled out the big guns of protest in Boston, J. J. McCarthy and Ted Mitchell began to fight back. They obtained statements from ministers, teachers, and other prominent citizens to the effect that these people liked the *Birth of a Nation* and recommended it to others for viewing. One of the ministers who made such a statement was the Reverend Pankhurst. These statements were printed in Boston newspapers.

A standard speech was worked out by our road show manager for some agreeing minister to deliver at a theater before the first performance of the *Birth of a Nation*. If a minister could not be secured, then the theater manager or J. J. McCarthy would deliver it. The following is a sample:
"Ladies and gentlemen:

"You are about to see—from the past— D. W. Griffith's film masterpiece, the *Birth of a Nation*. In time and technology, this picture is much nearer the Civil War than to our own time; indeed, it has been described as like the pictures of the immortal Civil War photographer, Matthew Brady.

"This noblest of all American films was made with passion and with dedication. It deals with an ugly chapter in American history —but a true chapter nevertheless. It has been, from time to time, called 'controversial.' In no case has the story proved unfactual.

"None of it reflects upon the great Negro race, a race which has contributed so much and continues to contribute so much to our culture in music, drama, politics, and philosophy. The picture does reflect, however, upon the white carpetbaggers who exploited the newly freed Southern slaves right after the war between the States. The Ku Klux Klan—as depicted in the picture—was disbanded shortly after the time of the story and bears not the slightest relation to the occasional sheeted bigots of today.

The Little Colonel (Henry Walthall)
is wounded in action.

61

"Be kind to this film. Treat it with tenderness and nostalgia. It will reward you by creating its own magic spell. Ladies and gentlemen —the *Birth of a Nation*."

While Griffith went to Boston, an irate Thomas Dixon was also marshalling his defense of the photoplay as well as a vigorous offense. He wrote many dispatches for newspapers and delivered a number of speeches defending the motion picture made from two of his books. His pride was more deeply wounded, perhaps, than was Griffith's, and he struck back at his racial critics with all the fury at his command in a treatise entitled, "The Action of the Negro Inter-Marriage Society Against The Play."

In a long article he wrote against the Jackson bill, purporting to restrict racial caricatures, Dixon said, "the chief source of character has always been and is today found in race and racial peculiarities.

"The masterpieces of the ages have been for this reason studies in racial traits. Hamlet is the analysis of the soul of a Dane. Othello is the study of the character of a Moor, the Merchant of Venice of an avaricious Jew.

"Two-thirds of the entire comedy output of the drama in America, both in films and in the spoken play, could be confiscated under such a law, and one half of the serious drama could in like way be destroyed. Shakespeare could be outlawed."

Dixon went on to list a number of plays produced on Broadway which had had strong racial implications, with no prolonged audience or press or NAACP protests. Why, then, Dixon asked, should minority groups protest about the *Birth of a Nation?* Did not a motion picture have the same freedom of expression and scope as a stage play?

The noted English journalist and publisher, Cecil Chesterton, brother of G. K. Chesterton, visited the United States at the time the *Birth of a Nation* controversy filled newspapers and magazines and was being discussed in drawing rooms, bars, and at sports events. In a dispatch for his newspaper, Chesterton wrote:

"When at the expense of a long and terrible war, the United States cleared itself of the guilt of slavery, it was (as it seems to me) clearly its right to decide, though certainly with due regard to the interest of the Negroes, whether and to what extent it would admit their freedom to the rights of citizenship. But to those who were intoxicated with the mere names of republicanism and democracy and had forgotten the philosophic theory which had underlain those names, this did not seem apparent.

Scene from the movie, showing confusion that followed the assassination of Lincoln.

Panoramic view of troop movements, showing Griffith's conception of the salient features of the Petersburg battlefield.

"Nor was abstract political philosophy the only force of which account had to be taken. As a matter of fact, the strongest of these men who carried through the Reconstruction were by no means actuated by such abstractions. To do them justice, they did not intend anything so wild as the idea that the Negro should rule the United States. Their intention, avowed with his usual courage and candor by Thaddeus Stevens, was that they should rule the United States with the help of the Negro vote."

Concerning the events which followed, Chesterton wrote, "Then came the scenes so vividly presented in Mr. Dixon's drama. An insane attempt to force Negro rule upon these citizens by and for whom the State had been built resulted in events which would be unbelievable if they were not matters of sober history. A grotesque riot of corruption and terror was ended only by armed conspiracy organized in defiance of the law, by which the government was at last beaten.

"It is astonishing how little is known of all this outside America. I frankly confess that I hardly knew anything of it before I came here. With the story of the first great Southern rebellion which failed, we English are tolerably familiar. Hardly one in a hundred of us has even heard of the second great Southern rebellion that succeeded. We all know how Lee surrendered to Grant at Appomattox. Hardly any of us know how twelve years later Grant's successor in the presidency surrendered to the ghost of Lee."

Chesterton was frank enough to state that he saw no definite conclusion to the controversy. "I pretend to come to no conclusion," he went on. "When the early abolitionists said that recognition of slavery by the State was a 'league with death and a covenant with hell,' I feel that they expressed my sentiments exactly. When Lincoln said that no commonwealth could exist half slave and half free, I am certain that he was right.

"When Mr. Dixon says that a Mulatto citizenship is too high a price to pay even for Emancipation, I know that if I were an American I should say the same. All that I can say as an Englishman, and I hope as a patriot, is that, conscious as I am of the many and heavy sins upon my country's record, I pray God that she may never have to pay for them as the American republic has paid for Negro slavery."

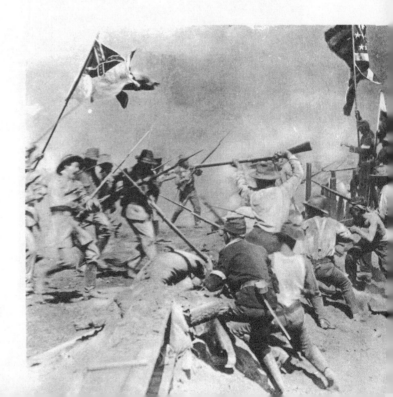

Confederate charge on the Union trenches.

HARRY HAS TROUBLE

WITH MUTUAL

Harry Aitken (left)
shakes hands with
Charles C. Hite, President,
Thanhouser Film Corp. (1913.)

The spring and summer of 1915 were exciting for Griffith, Dixon, Harry, and me, as well as for all those interested in our movie production and distribution companies. The world-wide success of the *Birth of a Nation* unloosed a flood of money in our direction and our heads whirled from our new found riches. Even Griffith and Dixon were amazed and delighted with the sudden prosperity. Both smiled happily when royalty checks were large. And in that first year, royalty and stock dividend checks came regularly.

Actually the year of 1915 was the happiest and most exhilarating of our lives, I think. It was a year in which Griffith, Dixon, Harry, and I were perhaps closer than at any other time. We were partners in the great forward movement of the motion picture industry, and we were acclaimed as men of foresight whose courageous pioneering had brought success. Who could blame us for dreaming of an exciting and still more prosperous future? Most others in our position would have done the same.

Griffith, of course, was more visionary than the rest of us. Restless, ambitious, he immediately set his heart on higher goals, and he tried to sell us on a costlier and more ambitious movie production program. While we wanted to concentrate on shorter pictures, he urged us to take advantage of the *Birth's* popularity and to finance longer and more lavish films.

When Harry came home to dinner one night, he told me, "Griffith wants a new contract with Majestic. He asks for a thousand dollars a week, plus special picture privileges and profits."

"Will he get it?"

Harry chuckled. "Why not? Two years ago he turned down Zukor's offer of a thousand dollars per week to come with us at three hundred a week plus Majestic stock. Now that the *Birth of a Nation* is a tremendous success, I suppose Griffith is entitled to this new contract. He's already talking about new pictures of the same type—expensive."

"Don't tell me we are going to have to try to hold him down again, like we did with the *Birth?*"

Harry shrugged. "Who knows? But we can't complain too much right now, so long as the *Birth* receipts keep rolling in. Roy, I have the feeling that we have turned the corner, that we are going on to greater pictures, bigger companies and more stability. Prosperity slows some people down—but not us. We've been too poor for many years. Now that we have more money to work with I think we'll accomplish more."

"I hope so. I just can't get over the habit of worrying about the weekly payrolls every Saturday. I still get that empty feeling in my stomach on that day."

"We have important work to do," Harry went on. "Freuler and some of the other Mutual boys are grousing. They're still angry because I censored some of the American Film Company's risque pictures a year ago and wouldn't distribute them through Mutual. They are also annoyed because they didn't get the distribution rights to the *Birth*. In fact, I think some of those fellows would be mighty happy if we stubbed our toes. But we won't. And I think I can handle Freuler."

"How? Mutual is one of the strongest film distribution companies in the country. We own a lot of stock in it yet, though not enough to control the company—now that Freuler's president instead of you. They've got us under their thumb, Harry. We need them to buy our Majestic, Reliance, and Keystone films for distribution since we no longer have film exchanges of our own."

Harry nodded. "True. But Mutual needs us too, Roy. They've got to have our pictures to supply theater clients."

"Perhaps," I agreed dubiously, "but don't forget they can buy some pictures from other independents in case we fail them. But we haven't any exchanges to sell to if Mutual sidetracks us."

"I know, but I'm already planning to handle that—in case."

"How?"

Harry smiled. "We thought we had an ideal situation, before Mutual started giving us trouble. We had two movie production companies, plus control of New York Motion Picture Corporation. And we had Mutual to distribute our pictures. When they deposed me and put in Freuler as president, I knew eventually we'd have to get some exchanges of our own."

"I was wondering when you were going to come out with that."

"And some day, Roy, we'll want our own theaters. We must think of that, too. We are

This picture was made in 1912 when I was president of Western Film Co., New York City.

close to it. When that day comes, then we can produce our own pictures, distribute them ourselves, and show them in our own theaters in key cities. We'll make three profits instead of one, and sell other distribution rights to independent theaters."

I groaned. "And I thought we were going to consolidate."

"We can consolidate more firmly by expanding," Harry pointed out. "The stronger we become, the better our competitive position. Zukor and Laemmle haven't thought of this triple profit idea yet. If we can stay ahead of them, then someday—"

"Someday, what?"

Harry lowered his voice and looked around. He didn't want even trusted Dunstan or Nellie to hear what he had to say. "Someday," he said, "if we get this triple system going, we'll be strong enough, perhaps, to take over any competitor."

I couldn't speak for a moment. Then, "Harry, this is worse than I dreamed."

"I can see it coming," Harry said prophetically. "Eventually, we'll have to take over most of our competitors, or they'll swallow us. I hope we're ready when the opportunity comes."

I didn't get much sleep that night. I haven't the genius for planning and administration that my brother had. I was not willing to work

Scene from *Intolerance*.
We lost $200,000
on this picture.

as relentlessly as he for a dream, day after day. I was more willing to settle for a full day's work somewhat above the average, so long as my road was sprinkled with some fun. Harry never seemed to need relaxation. Sometimes his intense daily concentration frightened me. He was a lonely man; he kept to himself most of the time. I was close to him only now and then—sometimes he came into my office at our quarters overlooking Times Square in a mood to talk. Once in a while he unloosed at dinner in our quiet apartment, and then I got a glimpse into his hopes and plans.

Now as I looked into the future I saw larger movie operations for us, requiring more financing on a huge scale, greater expenses and responsibilities. Could we, I wondered, stand up under the problems we would meet? Were we destined to have no time to build financial reserves or to enjoy life a little?

This was the period, too, when we began to have difficulty with Griffith. Flattered by public acclaim and adoration, he now became quite positive that all of his views about movie making, including financing, were above reproach. He resented any criticism of his producing plans and was hurt at suggestions of economy.

"Griffith certainly is in a hurry to start another picture," Harry told me as he came into the office one day. "He wants to expand that five reel special feature, *The Mother and the Law*, which he made for us while the *Birth* was being readied for release. He says it can

become a better picture than the *Birth* and a bigger box office hit. He wants to lengthen the old picture to include some parallel stories, a few from centuries past. The new picture will be called *Intolerance*."

"How does he know it will be a better picture than the *Birth?*" I asked cautiously.

"Well," Harry said softly, "you and I were wrong about the *Birth*, weren't we? No one except Griffith dreamed it would be an artistic and financial success on the scale it is."

"He didn't know," I said stubbornly. "He guessed and hoped."

Harry shrugged. "I figure we should let him try this *Intolerance* as his own special picture. He can produce it under his own company, Wark Producing Company. We can take an interest in the picture, and let him assume the big risk."

"How much will the picture cost?"

"About seven hundred fifty thousand, Griffith says."

I gasped. "That means over a million, if I know Griff. How much from us?"

"About two hundred thousand. He wanted four hundred thousand dollars, but I said no."

I got up and walked to the window and looked bleakly down Times Square. Harry came and stood beside me. "We've got to take a sizable interest in that picture—to hold Griffith. Zukor and others want him badly—especially since the *Birth* has established a new record in the industry. We don't want him to break his contract with us now. We can play along with him on this one picture."

"But two hundred thousand dollars!" I said. "That's about twice what it cost to produce the *Birth*. It's at times like this that I wish I were back in Chicago selling automobiles."

Although *Intolerance* was produced using material from *The Mother and the Law*, we didn't charge Griffith a fee. The plot of *The Mother and the Law* had been in part from a report of the Federal Industrial Commission, which realistically revealed the wrongs inflicted by a pious factory owner on his employees. The famous Stielow murder case was also drawn upon for material.

Mae Marsh, who played the part of the girl in the modern story section of *Intolerance*, says that San Quentin prison grounds were used by Griffith for part of the scenery in *The Mother and the Law*.

"We used the prison walls, the entrance and the yard in the picture," she wrote me. "The script called for the execution of Bobby Harron, although he was innocent of the crime charged. Bobby was smoking a cigarette when some real prisoners passed. One of them said, 'Buddy, if you'd drop that fag nobody would hold it against you.'

"While we were making the picture, the reports came in from all over the country about the great success of the *Birth of a Nation*. Mr. Griffith immediately decided that the big multi-reel pictures were the thing, and so he made *The Mother and the Law* as one part of a four cycle masterpiece."

The Mother and the Law was only a moderate success at the box office, but Griffith continued to brood about the story until the weaving of the parallel tales of the ages into the plot became an obsession. Into *Intolerance,* he poured his immediate profits from *Birth* royalties, plus our $200,000 investment, and he also obtained financing from friends. Bankers shied away from investing in the picture, however. They were not willing to take a chance on the long, colorful picture which Griffith described to them.

Since Griffith held controlling interest in *Intolerance,* he gave way to his innate showmanship and extravagance. He used his immediate cash and then got credit for much of his materials. He hired hundreds of players for vast crowd scenes, and he built a city of Babylon so sturdily that armies could march on its walls. There were also huge plaster elephants, lions, charioteers, and hundreds of dancing girls. One observer recalls watching eighty girls dressed as angels trying to balance themselves on wires to create a floating effect.

Miles of film were shot; in fact someone close to Griffith claims that the finished picture was eighty reels long, and that Griffith groaned when he had to cut it to twelve reels. No theater would run a longer picture.

Lillian Gish, one of Griffith's favorites, played the part of "The Mother Who Rocks The Cradle" in the picture. Other well-known players in the cast were Robert Harron, Monte Blue, Douglas Fairbanks, Alma Rubens, Bessie Love, Eric Von Stroheim, and Constance Talmadge.

Scheduled for release late in 1916, *Intolerance* was heralded as the greatest of Griffith's films. All of us looked forward to seeing how movie audiences would respond to the picture. Griffith and those who starred in the picture felt it would surpass the *Birth of a Nation* in box office appeal.

TRIANGLE

IS

FORMED

Gloria Swanson arranging her own lighting on a set during the early days at Triangle.

One spring morning Harry came into my office, and from the look on his lean face, I knew something was amiss.

"Freuler is balking at taking all Majestic and Reliance films for distribution through Mutual," he said sharply. "I think he wants to scare us, and to gradually become independent of our film output. Told me his American Film Company in California was producing more pictures for the Mutual program and that he wants a place for them."

I must have looked dismayed.

"Don't worry," Harry said. "I've expected this. I'm ready to organize a distribution company called Triangle. It will distribute Majestic and Reliance films and also those of the New York Motion Picture Company and of our subsidiary, Thanhouser Film Company."

I stared..

"I can get banker support for Triangle," Harry went on calmly. "Wall Street sees what the *Birth* is doing financially. Bankers are eager to work with us on good pictures. And I think Griffith, Ince, and Sennett will go along with this new company."

"But Harry, what have we got to offer them?"

"Stock in Triangle at a very low price," he said, "with time to pay for it. They can't buy into Mutual, but they can buy into Triangle. Have you ever seen a director who didn't yearn for stock in a producing company? We'll see how this bait works."

Events moved rapidly. Harry quickly arranged a meeting at La Junta, Colorado, with Griffith, Ince, Sennett and the Baumans and Kessels of the New York Motion Picture Corporation. In his briefcase, Harry carried unsigned contracts and verification of banking arrangements through Smithers and Company, a New York banking firm. All that was needed to make Triangle a reality was the signature of three of the greatest movie directors of the day, as well as the signatures of the owners of the New York Motion Picture Corporation, in which Harry and I also had stock.

I was worried, of course. We had invested $200,000 in *Intolerance* and I knew that in order to get financial support for Triangle, Harry had put up collateral, too. That meant our stock in Epoch Producing Company, Majestic, Reliance, etc.

If the three top directors and the Baumans and Kessels signed their Triangle contracts,

Ince's electric sign at Triangle's Culver City Studio.

however, we could meet the Mutual threat. If our associates didn't sign, if they remained with Mutual, or went with some other movie magnate, Harry and I would be relieved of Triangle financing—but could we fight our way to the top again without Griffith, Ince and Sennett?

While Harry went to La Junta, I sweat it out in our New York office. I think I realized for the first time since the *Birth* became a success, that so long as Harry and I stayed in this movie business, we could expect worry and trouble as well as one crisis after another. And always the competition would be waiting to take advantage of any weakness.

There would be battles ahead; not the kind that Griffith had filmed in the *Birth of a Nation*. These new battles would not be fought with guns, but with persuasion, money, and shrewd maneuvering. And the battles would be won by those men who could coldly out-guess competitors.

Walter Selisburg, one of our lawyers, and I were in my office going over some censorship reports when I got a long wire from Harry.

The La Junta deal had gone through. Triangle was now a reality. Griffith, Ince, and Sennett had signed their contracts. So had the Baumans and the Kessels. Triangle would be much larger than Mutual, Harry wired—and the Aitkens would have full control.

I handed the wire to Walter, who chuckled as he read it. "I knew Harry could do it." he said. "I have never seen him so determined and so enthusiastic as when we worked out those contracts for him to take to La Junta. You and he are entering a new development of the movies. For the first time since I have known Harry he has plenty of banker support for a deal."

"Yes," I said, "but don't forget Triangle will be costly to run if Griffith, Ince, and Sennett get their way too much. Remember, we have sunk two hundred thousand dollars in *Intolerance*. We can't afford any more investments like that."

The formation of Triangle Film Corporation certainly aroused excitement in the film industry. Harry's bold organizational moves in previous years were well known, but the suddenness of Triangle's birth amazed everyone. Many film people predicted that with Griffith, Ince and Sennett in Triangle under a stock holding arrangement, the new company could in time dominate the industry.

Triangle's charter was quite broad. Although authorized to produce pictures as well as to distribute them, Triangle did not produce immediately. Harry was content to buy Griffith, Ince, and Sennett productions for distribution under contract, from Majestic, Reliance, and New York Film Corporation. Profitable purchase rates were set up for these producers, based on a cost plus profit percentage. And since Griffith, Ince, and Sennett were now Triangle stockholders, they were so inspired that the motion pictures they made during the first year—1915-1916—were considered the best program films that theaters had ever enjoyed.

To allow directors to buy and own stock in a film company was a new development in the film industry. In the next few years a few other companies were to follow Triangle's lead, but on October 15, 1915, when Triangle was legally incorporated as a Delaware corporation, ownership of movie company stock was generally restricted to a few very enterprising men.

Again Harry had shown his genius for bringing various individuals and combinations together at a psychological time. Triangle began with sufficient banker support, top directors, and perhaps the biggest array of actors in the field.

69

Harry also moved quickly to set up film exchanges throughout the nation to handle the Triangle products. He had no difficulty in doing this, because so many film men wanted to tie up with the Aitkens and Griffith, Ince, and Sennett. Numerous film exchange men felt that Triangle was destined to be one of the most successful companies in the industry. At this period Triangle's star shone brightly in filmdom's sky.

In dealing with exchanges, Harry also set a precedent. Each exchange was new and was stocked only with new products. These exchanges were installed at small cost, with a release of two five-reel dramas, and two two-reel comedies per week. These were added to at the rate of two five-reel dramas and two two-reel comedies weekly. The constant supply of new films made many theater owners happy. To manage the new Triangle exchanges, Harry hired J. R. Naulty, who had handled the distribution of film for the General Film Exchanges a few years earlier. Under Harry's inspiration and Naulty's managership, the Triangle exchanges made money from the start and worried competitors.

Harry was busier than usual now, especially with administrative problems, but he was happier than I had ever seen him. True, Triangle owed huge sums to Wall Street, but Harry felt that since Triangle pictures were received so enthusiastically by film exchanges and theater clients, it would be only a matter of time before we could reduce those bank loans considerably.

Earlier in the summer of 1915, we had signed Douglas Fairbanks to a contract. Harry had given Doug an excellent contract: $2,000 a week for the first year; $2,500 per week for the second year and $3,000 a week for the third year. This was a tremendous salary at the time, but Harry felt that the energetic Fairbanks would be worth it.

The big salary, plus the fact that the *Birth of a Nation* was drawing huge crowds, finally convinced Fairbanks that his future could lie with the flickers—and so he left the stage. One clause of his contract specified that Griffith should supervise his pictures, for Fairbanks admired Griffith.

However, Griffith apparently did not like the boyish, enthusiastic Fairbanks. Perhaps this dislike stemmed from Griffith's feeling of inferiority with stage stars. And his coldness toward Fairbanks was to cause us trouble later on.

In the months that followed, Harry divided his time between New York and Hollywood. I took several trips out to the movie capital, but my office duties in New York cut short the pleasant Hollywood excursions. Since European film business was chaotic due to the war, we left Tom Davies in charge of London operations while I remained in the States to help Harry with our burgeoning movie empire.

When Harry got back from one Hollywood trip, he said, "Roy, there's trouble out there. Fairbanks is peeved because Griffith isn't supervising his pictures carefully enough, as the contract specified. Griffith has turned part of the supervising job on Fairbanks' films over to sub-directors."

"What's Griffith's excuse?"

"He's been busy, he says. He claims he looks in on Doug's rehearsals now and then. He promises to do better."

"How are Ince and Sennett?"

Harry frowned. "Another sore spot. They are famous now and hard to satisfy. They're envious of Griffith and want as many privileges as he gets. They have just as much Triangle stock as Griffith, but they are after more. We'll have to watch that situation with our directors. I've told all three separately

Douglas Fairbanks,
entertaining youngsters
at the Triangle Studio.

that the production of profitable pictures is our first aim. Somehow we've got to keep those three fellows reasonably happy and see that they don't get into one another's hair too much."

Despite their personal rivalry, Griffith, Ince, and Sennett managed to produce fine pictures for Triangle in 1915 and early 1916. Supplying scripts to Triangle were numerous well-known authors, including Mary Roberts Rinehart, Anita Loos, Octavus Roy Cohen, Arthur Stringer, Meredith Nicholson, Irvin Cobb, George Pattulo, Nina Wilcox Putnam and Samuel Hopkins Adams.

Players who had important roles in our Triangle pictures included Lillian and Dorothy Gish, Douglas Fairbanks, Alma Rubens, Belle Bennett, Dorothy Dalton, Charles Ray, Bobbie Harron, Olive Thomas, Bessie Barriscale, Bessie Love, Mae Marsh, Norma and Constance Talmadge, Gloria Swanson, William S. Hart, Frank Keenan, William Desmond, Mary Boland, Enid Bennett, Texas Guinan, Enid Markey, Louise Glaum, Pauline Starke, Margery Wilson, H. B. Warner, Sam De Grasse, Seena Owens, Marguerite Marsh, Monte Blue, Juanita Hansen, Wallace Reid, Mabel Normand, Ford Sterling, and Fatty Arbuckle.

A large number of these actors and actresses won stardom under our companies. Later—lured by huge salaries—some of them signed with other corporations, but they received their early training under our directors.

With such a roster of talented actresses, actors, script writers and directors, Triangle's output was attractive to hundreds of theaters. The future looked promising to us, and all of us were encouraged.

At this time, too, Harry realized that Triangle needed a theater on Broadway to show only pictures made by our companies. The Triangle board agreed with him. Since the Liberty was still showing the *Birth of a Nation,* Harry took a year's lease on the Knickerbocker Theater on Broadway. On September 23, 1915, the Knickerbocker opened under Triangle auspices with three features at a $2.00 top price. One picture was *The Iron Strain,* by Thomas Ince. Another was *The Lamb,* with Douglas Fairbanks, produced by David W. Griffith. And the third was *My Valet,* produced by Mack Sennett.

William S. Hart in a Triangle movie directed by Thomas Ince.

"Our directors can't kick about that," Harry chuckled as we dined at the Algonquin after the first show. "They all got top billing."

The manager of the Knickerbocker was a fellow named S. Rothafel, who later became known as the famous Roxy. He was a showman who had caught Harry's eye, and Harry was quick to hire him. Rothafel also opened a Triangle theater for us in Chicago.

As the movies began to attain stature by playing at top prices on Broadway to large crowds, Wall Street became more interested. Crawford Livingston financed the building of the Rivoli and Felix Kahn built the Rialto.

Then Messmore Kendall, who had been an investor in some of our syndicate pictures, built the famous Capitol Theater at 1639 Broadway. Just the other day, I found a letter in our files from Kendall to Harry, dated November 3, 1949. Kendall wrote:

"I have always considered that my visit to your California studios where you were making splendid pictures, brought about my decision to change my original intention of building legitimate theaters in New York to building the Capitol Theater for the showing of motion pictures. I am very happy that I did.

"Your sincere and devoted friend
"Messmore Kendall"

THE STAGE STAR
EXPERIMENT

As Triangle film productions poured from our California studios each week, we found that we needed larger quarters for the increased output. So we purchased an eleven acre tract of land at Culver City, California, between Los Angeles and Venice. Here we built a beautiful movie studio at a cost of approximately $500,000 and installed the hard working Thomas Ince and his players. Griffith and Sennett meanwhile remained at their Los Angeles studios.

The Culver City studio became one of the most famous of its type in the early days of the movies. Here some of Ince's greatest Western films were made, featuring William S. Hart. Sprawling over many acres, filled with buildings for production of motion pictures and their distribution, and with large storage areas for quantities of standard settings and equipment, Culver City made the nation gasp at its scope. Here again was proof that the motion picture had become big business.

Joe Weber of the famous
Weber and Fields comedy team.

In 1915, too, Triangle expanded in another direction. Harry conceived an idea which was destined to have a profound effect on Triangle's future and that of the other movie companies.

Observing the acceptance of our Douglas Fairbanks pictures and those of Frank Keenan, an Ince player, Harry realized that both these actors had come from the legitimate stage. De Wolfe Hopper, also a stage personality hired at $1,000 a week several months earlier, was presently finishing *Don Quixote,* a dramatic movie.

Why not contract outstanding stars of the spoken stage, vaudeville and musical comedy, Harry reasoned, and bring the art of the stage to the masses through the movies? Such a program, Harry believed, would be highly profitable to Triangle and would also set new standards for the film industry.

Harry was so enthusiastic about his stage star campaign that he convinced a rather reluctant Griffith and the rest of the Triangle board to permit him to try to contract more stage stars. To help him, Harry engaged the services of Arthur Klein, a well-known New York theatrical agent. By offering stage stars weekly salaries that dazzled them—$1,000 to $2,500 a week—Klein was able to contract for Harry the services of about sixty of the top stage players of the nation. The boldness of this venture startled even those accustomed to the rapid and often upredictable rise of the motion picture industry.

Reminiscing to a friend in 1952, Harry wrote about this part of Triangle's history, "Contrary to the general belief that the largest number of stage stars went into the talkies when they appeared in 1929, I took an even larger group of stage personalities with me to California in 1915.

"Among these were William Collier, Sr., and William Collier, Jr., Weber and Fields, De Wolfe Hopper, Douglas Fairbanks, Raymond Hitchcock, Frank Keenan, Willard Mack, Catherine Calvert, Orrin Johnson, Jane Grey, Harry Woodruff, George Fawcett, Crane Wilbur, Joe Jackson, Dustin Farnum, Charles Murray and others. I even imported Sir Herbert Beerbohm Tree from England to star in *Macbeth* and other plays."

Sir Herbert Tree received the unheard-of salary of $100,000 for six months' services.

Lew Fields received $2,500 a week and Joe Weber the same amount. Naturally such salaries raised costs of producing Triangle pictures to unprecedented levels. It was little wonder that many movie men, accustomed to a twenty-five cent admission price, gasped at the audacity of the Triangle plan.

Within a few months after the first Triangle pictures featuring famous stage stars were released, it was evident that the plan would not work out. Movie audiences apparently did not appreciate the type of play in which many of the Broadway stars were cast by Triangle directors. Furthermore, under the merciless glare of movie lights, many stage stars did not appear photogenic. On a semi-darkened stage in a legitimate theater, lights were kinder to aging actors and actresses.

Viewing the older, even though capable stage actors in classic roles, was also quite a shock for audiences accustomed to seeing pretty, golden-curled Mary Pickford, winsome Lillian Gish, pert Mae Marsh, innocent Bessie Love, Henry B. Walthall, Bobbie Harron, and others.

"I would have bet," a garrulous film salesman told me one day, "that those famous stage stars would become box office attractions. This shows how you can't guess right all the time. The money Harry's paying some of these people! He must have quite a bank account. You fellows are lucky the *Birth of a Nation* is still drawing the' crowds. What a money maker! Any chance to buy some stock in it?"

Confirmation of the disturbing news about the stage star venture drifted in from all parts of the country. The movie audiences wanted more Westerns from Ince, more love and family stories from Griffith. Sennett was not affected by the stage star experiment. His rollicking comedies were as popular as ever.

Harry assumed all the blame, as was characteristic of him. He was never one to pass responsibility for his actions onto others.

"It's my fault," he told me. "I was so certain this stage star program was right for Triangle. I had talked with many theater men, and most of them thought it a promising project. But it just didn't work."

"What now?" I asked nervously. "Our costs have gone up. Not only has our stage star experiment flopped, but we've been forced to raise many of our two hundred fifty dollar a week players to seven fifty or a thousand a week. And if we try to cut them, Zukor and the others will grab them."

"Don't rub it in," Harry said wryly. "I've got to ask our lawyers if we can cancel those stage star contracts, and how much it will cost us. We'll switch quickly back to full production on standard feature movies in which our younger players can play—and hope for a quick comeback."

"And our losses?"

Harry frowned. "We'll have to absorb them. But our regular Griffith, Ince, and Sennett pictures are still grossing well—some of them. We'll pay our losses out of those receipts."

"Thank Heavens, the *Birth of a Nation* is safe," I said fervently. "Epoch isn't in on the Triangle deal. It's a house by itself."

"I did the right thing when I didn't include Epoch," Harry said. "And Griff wanted to keep Epoch out."

I walked the streets of New York for a couple of hours that foggy night. How quickly conditions could change in the swift-paced, unpredictable movie business.

The promising stage star experiment had failed!

Harry had failed—for the first time in his movie career. And since Griffith had backed him in the stage star experiment—after initial reluctance—the famous director had, in a sense, also failed. This was a new situation for Harry and Griffith. Earlier they had had troubles. These were mostly financial. But now the failure concerned a misjudgment of what the public wanted. It was going to prove costly.

But then, no man can win all the time. You must expect to strike out once in a while, I reasoned. The thing to do was to watch out you didn't strike out with the bases loaded.

I buttoned my topcoat against the chilly fog and tucked my scarf closer about my neck. Well, we were not whipped yet. We still had a reputable movie organization, top players and directors. We would come back. Harry, Griffith, Ince, and Sennett would find a way to recoup our losses.

This was no time to give up. It was a time to take stock and fight. Perhaps fight for our financial lives.

I turned into a nearby night spot. I was hungry. It was time for a good meal and gay music to bolster sagging spirits. Then gird for the fight!

A MERGER

IS CONTEMPLATED

Entrance to eleven-acre plant
at Triangle-Culver City Studio,
now owned by M.G.M.

In mid-summer of 1915, too, our old distribution company, Mutual Film Corporation, began to experience output trouble. Deprived of Majestic, Reliance, and Keystone pictures, its management had to look elsewhere for enough films to supply its clients. Mutual received some films from Freuler's American Film Company, but this small firm could not turn out enough for Mutual's many clients.

Shortly before Harry had left Mutual to form Triangle, Mack Sennett had made a request through New York Motion Picture Corporation for an increase in salary for Charlie Chaplin. He was receiving $150 a week and wanted $450. Harry had presented the request to Mutual, but John Freuler, Felix Kahn, and Crawford Livingston were among those who turned it down. $450 per week was too high a salary for a comedian to earn, they felt. And since the Mutual board annually negotiated film distribution contracts with producers, they actually controlled the pay which movie players received.

John R. Freuler, Sidney Chaplin, and Charlie Chaplin signing contract giving
the famous comedian $650,000 for his year's work.

So Chaplin broke his contract with Keystone and was quickly signed for $1250 per week by George Spoor of Essanay studios. Mack Sennett was unhappy about losing Chaplin. In his place he hired Ford Sterling, who, along with Ben Turpin, Buster Keaton, Mabel Normand, Fatty Arbuckle, and the flashy Keystone bathing beauties, soon made Sennett forget about Chaplin. Sennett pictures continued in strong demand.

Essanay made a killing on Chaplin pictures during the next twelve months. By that time Freuler, Kahn, and Livingston had had their eyes opened. Freuler and his friends then lured Chaplin away from Essanay with a fabulous salary of $650,000 per year. The new Chaplin pictures were to be made by Freuler's American Film Company, which by this time had moved to California.

This tremendous increase indicates how movie star salaries skyrocketed between the opening of the *Birth of a Nation,* March 3, 1915, and the early part of 1916. Film players, directors, and financiers in the industry suddenly seemed to realize that the once struggling movie industry had become a profit-making enterprise with potentially fantastic earnings. Everyone scrambled to get a share of picture profits. As a result there was an unprecedented rise in production costs, principally in scripts, equipment and salaries.

Mutual did quite well with its Chaplin pictures, but one star could not keep its financial ship from sinking. Eventually, in the face of increased competition, Mutual quietly went out of business.

I think these events illustrate the far-reaching effects that followed the emergence of the *Birth of a Nation* as a film masterpiece. The tremendous crowds who were willing to pay $2.00 to see the twelve reel motion picture gave the industry the confidence and financial backing which was needed to organize on a sounder basis. It did not matter if the hurricane winds of competition were whirling about the heads of the Zukors, the Goldwyns, the Laemmles, the Foxes, and the Aitkens. It was quite evident that the American people were entranced by the movies and wanted more of them; the names of the producers did not matter.

Production was a jungle. The strong producers would survive; the weak would be slaughtered; but the industry would grow.

Triangle was in the midst of the fight. Added to our financing problems, we now experienced player trouble. The coolness between Douglas Fairbanks and Griffith worsened. Word got around that after witnessing Fairbanks' acrobatics, Griffith privately called him a jumping jack. This was the sort of jibe which hurt Fairbanks, who had learned his profession in the tradition of the stage.

Fairbanks complained so much about Griffith's treatment of him that finally Harry made plans to transfer Douglas from Hollywood to our old Yonkers studio in New York State, along with a few other players. To direct Fairbanks, Harry transferred directors Allan Dwan and John Emerson from under Griffith's wing.

Griffith didn't seem to mind, for he was too busy with his Triangle features. Harry also asked Griffith about Norma Talmadge, who had been signed a year earlier. She was a beautiful young actress with little experience. Griffith had cast her in a number of mother roles in which she did quite well.

Lee and Grant, as portrayed
in **Birth of a Nation**.

"Don't you think we could use her in some
younger parts?" Harry asked Griffith. "So
many fans like her."

Griffith shrugged and gave Harry a cold look
as though questioning his ability to judge
talent. "I've tried her in a number of pictures.
I don't think she has any special acting
ability."

So Harry took Norma Talmadge to the
Yonkers studio with Fairbanks and others.
There Dwan and Emerson worked hard to
turn out films that drew quite well and added
to the large number of quality standard pictures which Triangle was now issuing.

The fierce competition of movie companies
and the seriousness of Triangle's financing
program finally proved too great a strain for
the aging Charlie Bauman as well as Charlie
and Adam Kessel. When these early day
moviemen—who were also Triangle stockholders—saw film production costs rise and

movie star salaries go up, they suddenly got
retirement notions. Word went around that
they wanted to sell controlling stock in the
New York Motion Picture Corporation, which
they had founded in 1909. Harry and I had
had stock in the company for many years and
had financed their operations. We did not
want to see their stock go to others.

So, despite our heavy financial obligations,
Harry managed to borrow money in Wall
Street to buy a controlling interest from Bauman and the Kessels for approximately half a
million dollars.

"I had to do it to keep control of Ince
and Sennett productions," Harry explained to
a friend of ours at our apartment one night.

With acquisition of controlling stock in
New York Motion Picture Corporation and
its Kay Bee, Domino, Bison, Broncho, Keystone and other films, Harry and I now had
a firm grip on all companies producing for
Triangle, including Majestic, Reliance and
Thanhouser. This formidable producing group
was perhaps the strongest in the industry from
a talent viewpoint. We lacked only more financing to carry us until we had fully recouped
from the losses of the stage star venture.

One day Harry called me into his office.
"The banks are pushing us to pay up our loans
faster," he complained. "They expect miracles
in a short time. Why can't they be more
patient? They just haven't got the long range
view of the movie business." He frowned.
"They even want to put one of their men into
our office setup to check operations and advise economies, so we can funnel more pay-
ments to them."

"Well," I said, "perhaps we can learn something from them. We've been too busy all
these years to watch where every penny goes."

About this time I saw Douglas Fairbanks
quite often in New York on week ends. Doug
and I got along well. He admired the Leon
Bollee automobile I had brought over from
France. I frequently drove him around New
York and after I was certain he could drive
the car well, I let him take it to use on a few
dates.

"Roy, how about selling me the Bollee?"
Doug asked enthusiastically one day. "I like
it so much."

I shook my head. "I couldn't get another
like it now, Doug. They aren't making these
cars during the war for civilian use."

Ford Sterling (holding jewels) in the Keystone comedy, **Maiden's Trust**. He took ·Chaplin's place when the latter went to Essanay Film Co.

"Well," Doug said, disappointment on his handsome face, "when the war is over I'll still want to buy it. Remember that."

"All right," I agreed. "When the war is over!"

Some months later when Doug and I dined together, he showed me a telegram from Adolph Zukor, offering Doug $5,000 a week to join his company.

"It's a tempting offer, Roy," Doug said seriously.

"I suppose," I said, "but you have a three year contract with Triangle to work for us."

Doug nodded. "I have, Roy, and I like you and Harry. But my Triangle contract specified Griffith was to supervise all my pictures. He didn't like me so Harry took me to Yonkers. Now Dwan supervises my pictures. He's a nice fellow, and I like him, but—"

About ten days later, Doug showed me another telegram from Zukor. "I've got another offer, Roy. This time it's $10,000 weekly advance and fifty percent profit on all my pictures. You fellows had better do something about this!"

I left Doug about an hour later, and informed Harry of Zukor's offer. He was dismayed, for Fairbanks' Triangle pictures were doing well at the box office. The athletic, acrobatic star with the engaging smile was winning a large fan following. $10,000 a week! Our finances being what they were, we could not meet such an offer.

Doug broke his contract with us to sign with Zukor. I think he hated to do it, because he liked Harry and me. But perhaps he felt that the lure of $10,000 per week was something he couldn't resist. The court agreed with Doug that he could break his contract with Triangle —technically Griffith did not supervise all his pictures, as was specified. It was a slight provocation, but—

On November 11, 1918, when World War I ended, Doug telephoned me at the Beverly Hills Hotel in Los Angeles. Evidently he had heard I was on a trip to the Coast.

"Roy!" he shouted. "The war's over! Now will you sell me your Leon Bollee?"

As soon as I recovered from my surprise, I laughed. "Sure, I'll sell it, Doug. I promised I would. But it's not here. I left it in New York. I shipped only the Rolls out to Los Angeles. Want to buy it instead?"

"No, I want the Leon Bollee. Can you ship it out here?" So I sold the Bollee to Fairbanks for $2,500 plus shipping costs and he had great fun driving it around the California countryside.

Adolph Menjou, Adolph Zukor, and the famous violinist, Rubinoff.

THE

MOVIE GIANTS

MEET

25,000 yards of white sheeting were used to make the robes of the Ku Klux Klansmen in **Birth of a Nation**. Cowboys played the parts of Klansmen.

As the *Birth of a Nation* road shows continued to draw huge audiences, as well as praise from movie reviewers in many cities, other producers began to lengthen their motion pictures, and to spend more money on talent and scenery. The *Birth* was a model they kept in mind when planning and budgeting for their own forthcoming epic films.

One cold March day Harry came into my office overlooking Times Square, holding several sheets of paper. He pulled up a chair, sat down slowly and shuffled the papers. "Roy, Triangle is about ready for a plan I have had in mind for some time. I was even thinking of it when we bought New York Motion Picture Corporation's controlling stock."

"Not more expansion?" I asked anxiously.

"Well, I suppose you could call it that," Harry conceded. "Zukor, Goldfish, Lasky and DeMille are having the same growing pains and financing problems that we are. They can't always get enough capital to do what they feel they must do to stay in business in the face of intense competition. We have something they want—thirty-five well-established exchanges, three top directors, and two hundred fifty of the most talented film players in the industry. We've also got the most glamorous studio in the nation—Culver City."

Administration building at
Triangle-Culver City Studio.

I agreed, but I felt disturbed. Expansion always affected me that way.

Harry went on. "Who have they got to match Griffith, Ince, and Sennett? If Zukor and the rest could get those fellows they'd grab them tomorrow. But we have them sewed up on contracts that are pretty tight."

I said nothing. I know I looked apprehensive.

"This time we are going to aim for something really big, Roy," said Harry quietly. "A movie combine of Zukor's Famous Players, The Lasky Company and Triangle! Three big companies as one. Each of us needs the others. Who could beat such a well organized group?"

I was wide-eyed. Finally I managed to ask, "Suppose such a merger took place, Harry. Who would head it?"

Harry chuckled. "Well, I don't know, but I wouldn't turn down the job if it were offered to me. I've got all the details of how such a merger should come about. Now may be the time to get it done."

Negotiations for the movie company combine came about quickly. Miracle man Harry was able to get an agreement on a date at Culver City for a meeting of himself, Adolph Zukor, representing Famous Players, and Sam Goldfish, Jesse Lasky and Cecil DeMille, representing the Lasky Company. Twelve lawyers worked out preliminary contractual agreements, and this indicates that the Zukor and Lasky interests were presumably interested in merging with Triangle to form a combine which probably would have frozen out most competitors in a relatively short time.

When Harry approached bankers such as the Morgan group, he found them ready to cooperate. These bankers had money invested in Triangle, and in the Zukor and Lasky companies. They favored consolidation. A well-planned merger, many bankers thought, would safeguard their investments and also put the movie industry on a more businesslike basis.

The banker, lawyer, movie producer group that went to Culver City for the meeting were our guests and the meeting must have been congenial. Harry told me that Sam Goldfish shared a compartment with him on the train and at the Alexandria Hotel in Los Angeles. Harry even took our faithful English valet Dunstan along to minister to the needs of the guests. They got the red carpet treatment.

Harry had worked tirelessly to bring this merger to the point of contract signing. He had spent weeks selling competitors, bankers, and Triangle directors on the benefits of the idea. He was confident that the deal would be completed after brief discussions of contractual points. Newspaper reports publicized the merger negotiations.

Charles Hamilton (a leading actor in Keystone Cop Comedies), his wife (Rae Hamilton), and his father.

Raoul Walsh and his brother George on Triangle-Fine Arts set during filming of **The Smuggler.** George was a distributor of **Birth of a Nation.**

The *New York Journal of Commerce* published the following news item on April 16, 1916:

"Los Angeles, Cal.—It is reported that H. E. Aitken of the Triangle Film Co.; Adolph Zukor, of the Famous Players; H. B. Smithers of the F. S. Smithers & Co., and Samuel Goldfish of the Lasky Co. have conferred here on a plan for a consolidation of moving picture interests."

I later learned from Harry that he had enthusiastically outlined the advantages of such a merger to each of the participants. He exhibited Triangle records, showing all details of our operations, salaries paid to stars, film exchange policies, and other items. He felt he was talking to partners—not to competitors—and that the merger was now an actuality, except for the mere signing of contracts.

But the meeting adjourned without signing. Zukor and Goldfish said they would inform Harry within a few days of their decision. Zukor and Harry went back to New York, where Harry waited for Zukor's answer.

He waited a number of days. Then Zukor informed Harry he had decided not to join the Triangle merger. We soon learned the reason. Shortly, Zukor bought Sam Goldfish's interest in the Lasky Company and thus effected a merger of his own—without Triangle. That's how rapidly events moved in the booming movie industry in those days.

Some film people have since told me that one of the reasons why the merger of Triangle with the Zukor and Lasky interests did not go through was that Zukor, Harry, and Goldfish each wanted to be president of the combine, and that they could not agree on a candidate.

Others said that Harry insisted on withholding our highly profitable Western Import Company in London from the merger list. "This, I think, made Zukor wary; that was why the deal fell through," reports one informant.

Authors of other books about the history of the movies have hinted that Harry had been too naive in showing his competitors the intricacies of Triangle's operational plans before the signing of contracts. They say he should have played a more secretive hand of financing poker.

Whatever the reason, the merger idea was dead. Triangle once again stood alone, with its financing problems, in a field of ruthless competition.

And we began to feel the effects of the competition very quickly. Zukor already had Fairbanks under contract. Then Zukor and other producers began making attractive offers to more of our stars. As their contracts with Triangle expired, some of the stars went elsewhere. We could not meet competitors' salary offers. Within six months, more than two hundred of the Majestic, Reliance, Thanhouser, and Keystone players had gone elsewhere, and we were helpless to halt the trend.

"If only we had more financing," Harry moaned one day. "With so many of our stars leaving, we're in trouble."

"If we had the two hundred thousand dollars we invested in Griffith's *Intolerance,* it would help," I said bitterly.

Intolerance had recently been released to theaters, but was not doing as well as had been expected at the box office. Movie critics were lavish in their praise of its artistic qual-

ities, but extremely critical about its wandering story line. The public apparently agreed.

"Give the picture time," Harry said patiently. "It may still become a hit as people learn to look for the lesson it teaches. Then we'll get our money back, perhaps." Harry's eyes held a peculiar glow. I knew he was determined to save Triangle and to build it into a stronger financial structure if he could. Harry was never frightened of problems.

But the odds were against us. *Intolerance* did not make the profit its investors had hoped for. Our stars continued to leave us, and Griffith, Ince, and Sennett began to complain openly about the interruption of their producing programs caused by our difficulties in raising money.

I suppose it is only natural for people to flee a sinking ship. It was not long before David Griffith left us. He had little sympathy for our financial plight, despite the years we had spent building a movie empire from which he had taken handsome profits.

Griffith produced pictures independently for a short time, and then accepted an offer to join United Artists. This firm was a unique combine of the talents of Mary Pickford, Douglas Fairbanks, and Charles Chaplin. Each actor produced his own pictures, while United Artists took on the distribution program.

After Griffith left, Thomas Ince also got independence fever. He severed connections with Triangle when his contract expired, and entered the field as an independent producer, selling most of his pictures to Adolph Zukor. The only survivor of Triangle's "Top Three" directors—Mack Sennett—began to get restless, too. Finally, he informed us he was leaving Triangle and would produce independently as Sennett Comedies. The Keystone Cop name, of course, remained the property of Triangle.

To try to replace Griffith, Ince, and Sennett was a tremendous problem, it is true, but Harry and I were not downhearted. We hired a former Universal director, H. O. Davis, who was anxious to have an opportunity to produce without top brass supervision. Davis had the reputation of turning out good standard pictures with restricted budgets.

Harry and I then closed our Fine Arts Studio in Los Angeles, and also the Keystone Studio there. We consolidated all our California motion picture production at Culver City. This was retrenchment in earnest.

Gloria Swanson in **Haystacks and Steeples**,
an early Triangle picture.

I was placed in charge of Culver City operations for a number of months. "Roy," Harry said, "I can't leave New York right now. You know what we want. Work with Davis and keep me advised. I'll try to get out in a couple of months. This new setup ought to be much more economical for us."

So I sat in the executive chair of the big Culver studio, and it was a wonderful experience. I worked closely with Davis, expediting his requests. I found he was a practical man with a fine knowledge of movie making and he was dedicated to making good on this, his first top assignment.

Later our Culver studio became the headquarters of Louis B. Mayer of Metro Goldwyn Mayer, who received a million dollars a year salary. But at the time it was my office, and I put all my experience into the job. I had the knack of cooperating with others and enlist-

ing their support. Davis and I worked like a team. Within a short time he was turning out good standard films that proved readily salable to exchanges and theaters. In fact, Davis was able to produce his films for about $15,-000 each, which certainly was much less than what Griffith and Ince had been spending on each of their films the past year or two.

I was delighted with the way the new films were accepted, and so was Davis.

Davis also turned his talents toward making some Keystone Cop comedies, and they were creditable productions. For all his pictures Davis was able to attract many talented players who had not yet reached stardom, and he handled them with great skill. Part of my job, too, was to meet and talk with the players, trying to get them to remain with Triangle rather than jumping to other companies. Work like that requires a lot of persuasion.

Harry was too busy in New York with administrative and financing problems to come to Hollywood for a few months, but one day he saw several of Davis' productions in a screening room. He was shocked. The films were trim, low cost and fast moving, but they were not the lavish, spectacular pictures which Griffith and Ince had insisted on. Harry had been conditioned to the better quality pictures and found it difficult to accept the more realistic, stream-lined Davis productions.

He came to Hollywood, visited the studio and conferred with Davis. When Harry complained about the low cost type of picture Davis was producing, the director asked curtly, "Don't you like my pictures?"

Harry was honest. "No!" he said emphatically.

Davis quit immediately, and we were forced to hunt up a new director. Within a short time we hired and discharged two replacements.

I feel that when Davis left our employ, Triangle lost a good director. Had he remained in our employ and continued to make his economical pictures, I believe Triangle could have climbed out of its financial troubles.

But Harry was a hard man to please. Undoubtedly he had been spoiled somewhat by the reputation the more costly and elaborately staged Triangle pictures had achieved, and could not bring himself to accept what he considered an inferior product. I remonstrated with him, but I was overruled. Harry

Mary Pickford, who also got her start with the Aitkens.

knew what he wanted. His goals were always high.

Finally a day of judgment arrived. Smithers and Company stepped in and requested a change in Triangle leadership. Harry was deposed as president, and J. R. Naulty, a businessman, was named in his place. There was now little attempt made to produce new pictures. The only purpose of the new financial management of Triangle was to get as much money as possible for the bank investors by cutting costs and by reissuing old Triangle pictures and promoting current productions.

"There is now no hope for Triangle," Harry said sadly. "Bankers are not movie men. They have no creative imagination. Triangle competitors will now leave us behind. If only we could have held out a little longer. Then perhaps we could have taken in enough money to pay back some of those bank loans and get a new, top caliber director. But those bankers scare so easily."

"What can we do now?" I asked gloomily.

Harry did not reply for a moment. "We'll come back," he said finally. "It will take time, and perhaps we'll need a new company. But we can do it. We've faced tough problems before. Both of us are still young and we know the movies. And we still have controlling interest in the *Birth*. It is not mortgaged. Only Triangle is."

The collapse of Triangle as a major factor in movie production came rapidly in 1918. The beautiful Culver City studio went on the auction block, and became the headquarters for Louis Mayer of Metro Goldwyn Mayer.. Majestic, Reliance, Thanhouser, and New York Motion Picture Corporation went under. Their old films, some dating back many years, were sold at auction, as bankers collected every penny they could from Triangle assets. Our thirty-five film exchanges folded or were gobbled up by others. With our meager resources, Harry and I managed to buy only a few of our films at auction.

Thus tumbled the Aitkens' dream of movie empire which had started on a financial shoestring in the dusty nickelodeon days in 1905.

Why did we fail? Had we been too eager to grasp the many organizational opportunities that came our way? Had we both been too trustful of others?

To Harry and me, the collapse of Triangle was a soul shaking experience. From 1905 to 1918 we had poured our lives, our energies and our money into this fantastic movieland.

"We're still young," Harry kept telling me, his eyes dark-ringed. "We can come back. We know how to do it. We must not lose hope."

This was Harry's battle cry from that day on. He never gave up his dream of a comeback. He had supreme faith. It was this sort of faith and determination which had sustained him through several decades of a turbulent movie career.

Eddie Dillon, one of D. W. Griffith's directors in early Fine Arts days.

WE START ANEW

The films Harry and I bought at the sheriff's sale, plus additional films which we bought from the Tri Stone Company, a distributor, a few years later, enabled us to set up Aitken, Incorporated, at our family home in Waukesha, Wisconsin. This firm is still reissuing a number of Keystones and handling distribution of the *Birth of a Nation*.

"Well, Roy," Harry said, after we had set up business in Waukesha. "We are still in the movie business. These reissue films will continue to attract theater audiences for years. And the *Birth* distribution will help, too. Now we can start climbing the movie ladder again. We're in the forties. That's when life begins, they say."

Lovesick Union soldier (played by William Freeman) gazes at Elsie Stoneman (Lillian Gish).

Both of us laughed about that, but neither of us could forget the disappointment we tried to hide from each other.

In 1922, Hiram Abrams, president of United Artists, of which Griffith was a member, asked us to permit his company to distribute the *Birth of a Nation* to theaters, at prices below the $2.00 top for seats.

"We might as well do it," Harry told me. "*Birth* receipts at the two dollar top have fallen off steadily each year. United Artists has distribution rights with many theaters. They can get many bookings for us at low prices. Abrams thinks he can make a million dollars for us in cheaper priced theaters."

"Epoch would settle for a half million," I remarked drily. "Let him see what he can do."

Griffith, Dixon, and the rest of the Epoch board of directors gave their consent. Thus, after seven years of playing in the best theaters and at high prices, the *Birth* finally made its entry into theaters where the admission prices were fifty cents or slightly higher.

United Artists put a great deal of promotional effort into the *Birth of a Nation* when they booked it at low priced theaters in New York, Boston, Philadelphia, Chicago, and elsewhere. Immediately, too, the NAACP swung into action trying to boycott the film and to get injunctions against its exhibition.

The pressure of minority groups was strong, so much so that some censorship boards listened to their arguments. The following deletions in the film were demanded when United Artists wanted to show it in New York, and this indicates the stiffening of censorship over what it had been in 1914 and 1915.

"Dec. 20, 1922
"New York City, N. Y.
"Dear Sir:

"We have gone over the suggested eliminations in the *Birth of a Nation* and have decided upon the following eliminations which you will please make before the picture is shown in this state. If you will advise us by letter that these eliminations have been made in all prints to be exhibited in New York State, it will not be necessary to return the same for rescreening:

"*Act 1:* Shorten view of mulatto woman on floor, tearing dress waist and with dress off shoulder.

"If in the picture, eliminate scene of

Stoneman kissing and embracing mulatto.

"*Act 2:* Suggest that authority be given for quotation: 'to put the white south under the heel of the black south.'

"Eliminate actual scene of whipping Negro.

"Eliminate scene of Negro removing shoes and sitting at table in Senate in bare feet.

"After subtitle: 'We will destroy the white south under the heel of the black south.'

"Eliminate closeup of Negro's face.

"Eliminate scene where Negro Gus lays his hand on girl.

"Eliminate all closeups of Negro Gus chasing the girl.

"Eliminate view of dead girl in bier.

"Change subtitle: 'This flag bears the red stain of the blood of a Southern woman.'

"Eliminate all but one scene of the master in chains.

"Shorten scene between Lynch and Elsie. Show but one view of Lynch embracing Elsie.

"Eliminate all views of Elsie actually gagged.

"The reasons for the above eliminations are that they are 'indecent,' 'immoral' and 'would tend to incite crime' and some of them are inhuman.

"Very truly yours,
"George H. Cobb, chairman
"Motion Picture Commission
"State of New York"

Hiram Abrams was enthusiastic about the *Birth of a Nation* receipts that first year under the United Artists distribution wing. He then offered me a job—to visit his district offices and theaters where the *Birth* was showing, to help owners and managers to advertise and otherwise promote the picture. My first-hand experiences of the way Ted Mitchell and J. R. McCarthy had handled the road shows helped me to guide theater managers to excellent promotional ideas.

There was only one Mitchell exploitation stunt I did not dare to use; that was the one where a group of white-clad horsemen representing the Ku Klux Klan, would ride down the main street of the city in which the *Birth* was showing, yelling loudly and finally pulling up in front of the theater.

Later that year Abrams recalled how I had

Wilfred Lucas and Hedda Hopper.

organized the Western Import Company film exchanges in Europe, and he then sent me to England to help the English theater managers in promoting the *Birth* as well as other United Artists offerings.

I enjoyed this assignment and was happy to be back in England. I had always admired the English for their discipline and distinctive way of life. I was pleased, too, to return to the habit of having tea at four—even in business offices.

Nevertheless, I could not help but feel depressed at times, too, because I was no longer a part of a progressive team of movie producers who had seemed destined for noteworthy film achievements. All that was gone. I was now only an employee of United Artists.

However, I did not allow these nostalgic moments to rob me of the satisfaction of work that I loved—being connected with the movies in some capacity.

One day as I was leaving London for Paris to arrange some United Artists film bookings, I read in a British newspaper that Douglas Fairbanks and Mary Pickford were honeymooning in Paris. They were stopping at an exclusive French hotel and were being besieged by curious movie admirers.

85

After I had concluded my film business in Paris, I went to Doug's hotel. To get into the lobby I had to push my way through a jammed crowd seeking admittance. Finally I reached a guard who sent my card up to Doug and Mary's suite.

I waited about thirty minutes, then I was told to come forward. I waded through a crowd of guards and secretaries, and later in the Fairbanks' suite, I met Doug and Mary.

They seemed happy to see me. Doug was delighted to know that I was with United Artists, and we chatted about the early days of the film industry and about that year of 1911 when a determined little Mary, under a contract to our Majestic Film Company, made *Little Red Riding Hood* and *The Courtship of Mary*.

"I'll always remember driving your Leon Bollee around New York back in 1915, Roy," chuckled a graying, but still boyish Fairbanks. "I didn't have enough money to buy one, and Harry and you were urging me to sign up for a film role. I didn't think much of movies then, but look what they've grown into."

Joseph Henabery, who played the part of Abraham Lincoln in **Birth of a Nation**.

As I walked back to the United Artists Paris office, I felt happy that Harry and I had had a part in giving these great film stars a start in the infant motion picture industry. They were wonderful people, and they were the idols of millions. But I could not help wishing that the Aitkens had had similar good fortune.

The United Artists organization handled the world wide distribution of the *Birth of a Nation* for Epoch Distributing Company from 1922 through 1926. Then, as the market for the famous silent picture dwindled, they turned it back to Epoch. We didn't make the fortune through United Artists distribution which Abrams had predicted, but the picture did gross a considerable sum under their management. However, by the time the theater owners took their advertising costs and percentage cuts out of the gross, and the United Artists its percentage as distributor, the share left for Epoch Distributing Company was considerably smaller.

For eleven years, this great silent motion picture had played to millions of people and grossed a lot of money at the box office. It had provided Epoch stockholders with excellent dividends on their investment; but it was evident now that the days of big earnings for the picture had vanished unless something entirely new and attractive was done to stimulate additional interest.

"I don't know right now what we can do about it," Harry told me when I came back to Waukesha after my European job with United Artists had ended. "We'll still get bookings from theaters now and then on the *Birth,* but we may have some mighty lean years!"

His prediction became a fact. And, handling the *Birth* again, we uncovered a rather irritating situation.

In the early days of the motion picture industry, most focus, of course, was on production. Practically everyone engaged in making motion pictures and getting them on the market, and in staying ahead of competition, neglected to keep accurate, detailed records of films in transit, films handled by exchanges, etc. Many prints of each picture were made so as to keep all exchanges supplied with prints for immediate use.

As a result, unauthorized prints of films in transit were sometimes made by unscrupulous people. In other cases, prints were said to

be lost and later some of them reappeared on the open market without our knowledge. The *Birth of a Nation* and all other films can be protected by copyright for twenty-eight years. Then copyright protection can be renewed for another twenty-eight years. Therefore, anyone wishing to exhibit a *Birth* film in a theater for profit during the terms of the copyright is required to obtain legal permission from the owner.

"Roy," Harry said one day, looking up from a letter, "there must be a lot of duplicate *Birth of a Nation* films floating around. Here's another report of the *Birth* showing in Ohio. We didn't authorize that one. I'll have to write the manager of the theater to find out where he obtained that film."

I have encountered this vexing situation many times in trying to get bookings for the *Birth* from 1927 through 1962. It is difficult to track down the offenders. Such unauthorized showings are film pirating, to be sure. If we catch such people, we can get payment for the use of the film. But there must be many cases that we never hear about where these "dupe" or pirated films are being used. I suppose Epoch Distributing Corporation has lost tens of thousands of dollars in this manner, but we do not have a national network of spotters.

During the late 1920's our paths crossed again with that of our former director, David W. Griffith. For a number of years his directorial star had been dimming. While he was still regarded as the artistic master of American films, his art had not led him into new fields since the production of the *Birth of a Nation* and *Intolerance.* The film industry now generally agrees that these were his greatest pictures.

After he had left Triangle to become an independent producer, Griffith made a num-

ber of pictures. The better known of these were *Hearts of the World, Broken Blossoms, Way Down East,* and *Orphans of the Storm.* Of these, only *Broken Blossoms* was an artistic and financial success.

Griffith became discouraged, bitter, and morose. When he met us accidentally in the Algonquin Hotel in New York in the late twenties, Harry and he immediately began to talk about the *Birth of a Nation.*

The possibility of a remake of the *Birth* from beginning to end, intrigued both of them. I sat in a lobby chair listening to them talk, these men whose partnership had led to great achievements for both, and who were now both faced with the task of regaining lost laurels.

87

The South Carolina Cavaliers depart for the war.

"I think it would go, D. W.," said Harry, with old friendliness. "The script would need to be rewritten, but perhaps we could raise some money for it, if they knew all of us would be together on the remake."

"But it would cost at least a million," Griffith said gloomily. "Where would we get that kind of money? None of us are as rich as we once were." There was a sneer in his tone.

It was true. None of us were rich. Relatively speaking, we were poor, all of us. Griffith was having a difficult time getting backing for a picture named *Abraham Lincoln* that he was planning to make to recoup lost glory and wealth. Thomas Dixon was practically broke. He wrote letter after letter from his North Carolina home asking what we were doing to promote the *Birth* so he could get more money. He needed it badly, he wrote.

Six months later there were rumors of sound pictures. Quietly, experimentation had been going on, and now movie officials indicated sound would shortly be practical. It could change the entire industry. Imagine—no more silent pictures!

Griffith was thinking about sound, too. In a letter which he wrote to A. H. Banzhaf, an Epoch director, in August 1929, he said: "Dear Mr. Banzhaf:

"The enclosed letter is self explanatory. I told Mr. Frank Woods that I would write you so that you could get this before the Epoch Producing Co.

"They put on the *Birth of a Nation, Intolerance,* and *Broken Blossoms* in these revivals in Los Angeles, and all of them did considerable business. Strange to say, the revival of Charlie Chaplin's *The Kid* and his other pictures were not a success. I understand that the only other picture that did any real business was one of Valentino's. The people lined up in double rows for blocks at the first showing of our pictures, so they put them on again for another day of the second week when they did the same business.

"My information was they did as much with the *Birth of a Nation* in a day as the very unsuccessful Film Guild House played in a week. I think there is no doubt that if the *Birth of a Nation* were synchronized, so the

William S. Hart, Enid Markey, and
Barney Sherry in **Evening Clothes.**

small towns could hear the music, you could get a lot of money, I am sure. Of course, here they only had an organ which will not play the score; merely did the best they could.

"Has Aitken thought of synchronizing the *Birth?*

"And what have you done about the California rights? Is there no contract in existence? Of course, you must remember that I own fifty percent of the California rights with Clune. With or without a contract, this percentage belongs to me. We should make some arrangements because I am sure there is a nice little piece of change waiting out here for the *Birth,* particularly if it is synchronized.

"I am progressing with the researching on the Lincoln picture, which has the possibilities of an epoch-making picture. If I can only get it put on without lame brain interference, I think there is a fortune in it.

      "As Ever

       "D. W. Griffith"

The Aitkens were also thinking about sound. We were excited by the prospect of sound on the *Birth,* but we knew that there were many difficulties to overcome.

First, the cost of dubbing in sound would be high but not as high as the cost of filming a new *Birth.* The motion picture industry had agreed on a projection speed of ninety frames a minute, while the silent film speed was seventy frames per minute. This presented a problem. Griffith had purposely filmed the Ku Klux Klan riding scenes in the *Birth* at a fast speed to add excitement. Now with the sound speed at a different pace, a sense of unreality might arise from showing the old silent pictures with dubbed in sound. And there would be a big demand for synchronizing silent pictures in hopes of making more money. This would send costs to high levels every month.

"We've got to investigate," Harry said as we discussed the matter. I'll contact Griffith and Dixon on it. And we'll have to try to find a way to raise some money. Who knows, Roy, this synchronization of the *Birth* may send profits on the picture rolling in again? We've got to do everything we can to start the program going. This project may put the Aitkens back into the movie business on a big scale."

Scene from Triangle-Keystone production,
Haystacks and Steeples. Bobby Vernon is
kissing Gloria Swanson's hand.

THE COMING

OF

SOUND

Griffith and Dixon were eager to agree to the plan for dubbing sound onto the *Birth of a Nation* film. Like us, they were quite excited at the prospect. Sound pictures had gripped the imagination of the movie audiences, and producers were rushing preparations to launch sound films and to synchronize popular silents. Synchronization of the *Birth* silent version would mean adding special music to the edge of the film.

Harry and I met Griffith and Dixon at the Algonquin Hotel in New York, the scene of many of our former conferences with bankers, authors, agents, and movie stars. It had been a long time since Harry and I had had a conference with Griffith and Dixon, and I think all of us were quite happy at the thought we might be partners again in an enterprise that had promise of bringing profit to each of us. We had dinner and discussed the changing movie scene and the furor raised by the advent of sound. Gone were our memories of the mistakes of the past, the lost opportunities, and the differences we had had during the Triangle split up. Now all of us looked to the future.

The *Birth* had been the greatest of the silent pictures. It had thrilled millions and had been the best moneymaker of the silent era. Synchronized, this picture might again gross large receipts—sixteen years after its 1915 debut. Just the thought of it made my blood race.

"Harry," Griffith said during the dinner, "we face a financing problem again. Have any of us money to invest in the *Birth* synchronization?"

"I can't invest any money," Dixon said dourly. "Haven't had a decent income in years."

"Well," Griffith went on, looking at Harry, "do you think you and Roy can raise enough money to handle the *Birth* synchronization?"

Harry looked squarely at Griffith. "We'll try," he said. "We still have connections. I'll get estimates on the sound dubbing so I'll be able to tell investors what the project will cost. Perhaps a hundred thousand dollars, I suppose."

"We'll be lucky if it doesn't cost two hundred thousand," Griffith said glumly. "Costs are going up steadily."

No one said anything for a moment, but I knew what was going through everyone's mind. The *Birth* had cost $110,000 to produce just sixteen years earlier. Now it might cost twice that amount just to add sound effects to the picture. Costs had gone up—but opportunity still beckoned, for those who took risks, and who were willing to face failure.

When I viewed the material on display at the exhibit of the State Historical Society of Wisconsin, I wished Harry could have been there with me to share the honors.

COSTS

I could not help interjecting, "I hope we don't have the difficulty raising this money that we did with the *Birth* finances back in 1914. We sweat blood on that one—all of us."

Even Griffith smiled wryly at that remark.

But we did have trouble raising the money to synchronize the film. Through the years the NAACP and other minority groups had harassed the *Birth*, wherever it was shown. Such facts caused investment money to shy away.

"Why try to revive such a controversial picture by putting sound to it?" many moneyed men said. "The investment risk is too great."

"A great picture is a great picture," Harry told one doubting film man. "It should not be suppressed just because minorities don't like it. If synchronization will make it a better picture for movie goers to see, it should be done."

There followed six months of effort to sell investment people on the idea of financing the synchronization of the *Birth*. Harry was still an influential man. He had hundreds of friends among bankers, industrialists and theater men. They recognized him as one of the pioneers who had done much to build the industry, and they gave him credit for this. But to invest money to dub in sound on the *Birth* film. That was too big a gamble. Harry did get some token pledges, but not nearly enough to finance the synchronization project.

Finally, Harry met George Kemble, a former theater man from Brooklyn. Affable, ambitious Kemble had rented and shown the *Birth of a Nation* in his Brooklyn theater. In fact, he was a *Birth* fan.

Call it fate, perhaps; Kemble was deeply interested in the Birth synchronization project. He would get cost estimates, he said, and if the project wasn't too expensive, he would get the money to finance it. He asked for a fifty-fifty split on profits. And he got it. Why not? What could we lose?

A jubilant and exhausted Harry came back to Waukesha. "We didn't give up, Roy, and we've got a backer. Kemble will get a five year contract if he raises money to swing the deal."

Kemble raised the money—about $150,000, and Griffith was engaged to edit the *Birth* for synchronization. How he hated to cut the silent picture, but, at Kemble's insistence, he finally eliminated many scenes to reduce the film's running time.

Harry worked closely with Griffith at this period. He said that the older, graying Griffith had lost some of his arrogance and was more willing to cooperate. Griffith's directing career was fast drawing to a close at this time and undoubtedly his editing of the *Birth* helped temporarily to lift him from his depression.

The St. Charles Theatre advertisement for a showing of **Birth of a Nation** after sound was added.

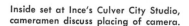

The Western Electric Company handled the actual synchronization task under Kemble's and Griffith's supervision. Later, the firm was awarded an Oscar for the technical excellence of the job. The musical score, well known to Americans, carried parts of *The Perfect Song,* for which we got publisher clearance. Finally, in less than a year, the synchronized version of the *Birth* was ready for premiere showing at a San Francisco theater.

Griffith, Harry, and I were there, along with a number of interested film men. Thomas Dixon wrote that he could not afford the long trip West.

I was excited as the sound film began to show on the screen. When the modulated music filled the theater, and blended with the action and mood of the picture, my heart beat fast and my hands gripped the arms of my seat. So much depended on this *Birth* venture. Would the synchronized version be satisfactory? Was it the answer to a new movie career for Harry and me—and perhaps for Griffith and Dixon?

I can't explain it, but listening to the synchronized *Birth* film was almost like watching a different picture. The music was impressive, and the speed of the picture was greater than that of the silent version. These factors contributed to my impression, I am certain.

There wasn't too much crowd reaction, although I could see that people were interested throughout the show. But there were not the wild, unrestrained cries that had greeted the film at its first showing in New York in 1915. Audiences had become more sophisticated.

After the show, as we sat in the theater office, Harry said, "It takes five minutes before one gets used to the faster speed of the synchronized version. But to me, it's a wonderful picture, and always will be."

Griffith agreed. "It can't quite compare with the silent version, but it's still a dramatic picture. I hope the public likes it. To millions who have not seen the silent version, the synchronized *Birth* will have tremendous appeal."

"It's got to sell well," Kemble said quietly. "All my money is tied up in it, as well as the money of many friends. We want our money back—plus."

The synchronized version got quite a few bookings the first few months, but the volume of business was only a whisper of what the silent picture had done back in 1915. Kemble, Harry, Griffith, and I soon realized that while the new version would always hold interest in some states and get bookings it would not become the profit-maker we had hoped.

To this day, the synchronized version gets billing at art and other theaters that schedule it. But in many cities when advertisements appear that the *Birth* will show, minority groups swing into action. By letter, by brochure, by word of mouth, they urge their members to protest against the exhibiting of the picture. And these protests have sometimes been very effective. Minority groups certainly have the right to protest against the *Birth* or any other motion picture they do not like, but we, who own the pictures, also have the right to try to get suitable audiences for the films, so long as they violate no moral code.

In recent years, an increasing number of art and drama classes at colleges and universities have begun to rent the *Birth of a Nation* film to exhibit to students. Professors lecture on the *Birth's* place in the history of the art of the movies. They also discuss the social effects of the controversy over the picture since 1915. To accommodate this demand, Harry and I made quite a few 16 millimeter prints of the film, since University projection machines do not handle the 35 millimeter theater size film.

Norma Talmadge starred with Douglas Fairbanks in a number of films produced at our Yonkers studio.

Kemble ran into financial difficulties in distributing and promoting the sound version of the *Birth of a Nation*. In fact, his financial maneuvering finally brought him into court. So within a short time Harry and I had to cancel the contract to protect ourselves, the reputation of the *Birth* film and the other investors. Kemble had great plans, but he used questionable judgment in his promotion and had to suffer for it.

The sound version under Kemble's management made little profit for anyone.

"I wonder," Harry mused one night in the fall of 1937, "if this would be the time to try to promote a complete remake of the *Birth of a Nation*—new photoplay, new actors, but perhaps with the same director—David Griffith."

"We couldn't stand the strain!" I cried in alarm. "We're both getting a little gray."

Harry smiled. "As a moneymaker, the silent version is finished and the synchronized version will bring in only limited income. But if the *Birth* could be remade entirely, in a modern way, it might make a smash hit as it did in 1915. The drama is still there in the picture. So let's bring it up to date."

"Let's not try it, Harry," I pleaded. "Let's stay here in Waukesha and be content to reissue the films we still have. We own Keystone and Triangle pictures that still have a call now and then. And the *Birth* synchronized version plays occasionally."

Harry shook his head. "It isn't enough. And the *Birth* is too great a picture to be allowed to fade away. I have a hunch that with the right touch, the *Birth* could again make audiences gasp."

I sighed. I knew there would be no stopping Harry. "We couldn't get the money to finance a remake," I said. "Look how lucky we were to get Kemble to finance the synchronized version. There may not be another Kemble for the remake."

Nothing I could say would deter Harry. "I'll write Griffith and Dixon to see what they think. They may have some ideas."

I must admit that seeing Harry's determination, and catching some of his enthusiasm, I began to feel stirred up, too. You can't chase a fantastic dream most of your life, hold it, and then lose it, without hoping you can capture it again. Harry and I were getting older; if we were to try for a *Birth* remake, this was the time, not later.

A bevy of Mack Sennett's Keystone Comedy beauties in a scene from **The Dark Room Secret.**

CONCLUSION

By the mid-thirties, Griffith's picture direction opportunities had become limited. *Abraham Lincoln,* the film in which he had placed so much hope for an artistic and financial comeback, had not drawn well at the box office. Film men were now saying more frequently that the old master had definitely lost the "touch," that modern movies had outpaced his older and often more sentimental approach. As this news got back to Griffith, he became morose. He was living at the Hotel Astor in New York at this time, seeing few people and trying to rewrite some of his unsold plays.

When Griffith got Harry's letter about the possibility of a *Birth* remake, he was quick to answer. In fact, he sent a wire:

"Suggest renting office and securing staff for budget and preparing story. Hope to get staff that made budget on *Gone With The Wind.* Could get entire groundwork of new picture laid in a month. Cost would not exceed $2,500."

This telegram indicated clearly that Griffith was excited about the idea of remaking the *Birth of a Nation,* and that he was eager to begin work on the project. It meant, too, that he had confidence in the Aitkens again. He felt that somehow we could raise the money for this project, just as we had raised the money to get the *Birth* silent version started in 1914.

Dixon answered quickly, too. Ailing, and in need of money, he liked the remake idea and wrote he wanted to do the rewrite on the photoplay. His price was $10,000, plus a royalty interest.

Harry whistled when he read Dixon's letter. "The same Tom," he said. "His financial ideas haven't changed. He's the man to do the rewrite, though. No other."

As Harry plunged into the work of arranging a meeting in New York with Griffith to discuss the *Birth* remake and the financing, I remained in Waukesha to handle the work of keeping the reissue of our films going steadily. They brought in some revenue seasonally, and we needed all of it now to handle the preliminary expenses connected with a *Birth* remake.

Two days before he left for New York, Harry visited friends in Milwaukee. When he came back to Waukesha, he said, "Roy, I actually got some promises from Milwaukee men that if the *Birth* remake idea gets New York support, they'd invest in it, too."

"Look, Harry," I cautioned. "Don't get too excited about the prospect. Let's take it slow this time."

Memorabilia of early movie days, displayed in State Historical Society of Wisconsin Movie Exhibit (1964).

Harry smiled tolerantly. "The other deals, like the synchronized version, didn't have the appeal the remake idea has, Roy. Movie men remember what the silent picture did in 1915 through 1922. They'll want to be in on the remake in case it hits a bonanza like that."

"I hope so," I said. "I hope so."

Harry and Griffith met in New York for four days. They didn't need to rent an office. They had plenty of time to talk in a hotel room and lay their plans. They decided that Harry should visit financial interests in New York and begin raising money. Meanwhile, Griffith would phone Dixon and get an outline of how the new photoplay would run; this would help Harry sell the idea of the new *Birth* to prospective investors.

"Griffith and I reached an agreement," Harry wrote me. "He will direct the picture and select the stars to play in it. It is my job to try to get enough money raised so we can begin work on the picture."

I noted that Griffith apparently did not offer to help Harry raise the money. Once again, as in 1914, Griffith seemed content to let Harry do the brunt of the work—getting the funds. Stripped of his confidence and most of his arrogance, Griffith perhaps realized that he had nothing to offer investors—that the success of the venture depended on Harry's sales ability.

After several weeks of intensive selling, Harry had pledges of about $100,000, but it was only a fraction of what was needed to make a picture which would compare with the scope of the silent version.

"It's not enough," Griffith said bitterly. "We should have at least half, or four hundred thousand dollars, before we begin such a long picture."

Sorrowfully, both Harry and Griffith abandoned the *Birth* remake idea for the moment. Griffith went back to his lonely hotel room to rewrite his plays, while Harry came back to Waukesha.

"I've got to pay Dixon twenty-five hundred dollars out of my own pocket for his work on that photoplay," Harry told me. "The rest of the promised sum of ten thousand dollars, he'll just have to forget. He must share with us in this loss."

I shook my head but said nothing.

"I still haven't given up on a *Birth* remake,"

Harry said stubbornly. "But this time we'll try to get an established producer to finance it, with a percentage to us. Then we won't have to worry about raising a large sum of money. I should have thought of that angle a long time ago. I hope I live long enough to see such a deal go through."

The years sped by. Harry and I began gathering data about our long movie career. "While we are waiting for some producer to buy the *Birth* remake idea," Harry said, "we can start writing a book. Let's make a list of the firsts we have achieved in the industry. That ought to be interesting."

So we made a list of the highlights of our career:

We established the first national film distribution company—Mutual Film Corporation —in 1911.

We were the first motion picture company to publish a series of full page advertisements in the *Saturday Evening Post*—1912—extolling Mutual pictures made by the three greatest directors of the era, David W. Griffith, Thomas Ince, and Mack Sennett.

We were the first American film company to set up foreign film exchanges (1911) headquartering in London, with branches at Copenhagen, Berlin, Paris, Rome, and other cities.

We financed and distributed the first twelve reel motion picture, the *Birth of a Nation,* which set new artistic standards for the motion picture industry.

We were the first motion picture company with a continuous producing and distribution system of our own. Triangle bought the films produced by our leading directors and rented them to our own film exchanges, which distributed them to theater owners, and to managers of a few theaters which we owned.

We were the first movie company to produce a weekly news and style show. Featuring Norma Phillips, the Mutual Girl, the show was viewed by millions of women every week and led to the development of news reels preceding feature pictures.

We were the first movie company to develop into stars such fine performers as Douglas Fairbanks, Gloria Swanson, Charles Chaplin, Norma and Constance Talmadge, William S. Hart and many others. Players such as the Gish sisters, Henry Walthall, Mae Marsh, and Mary Pickford got their start in pictures at

Biograph, but they reached stardom in Aitken financed companies.

During the Thirties, too, Harry was a key figure in establishing the film library of the Museum of Modern Art in New York. To the museum he donated a master print of the silent *Birth of a Nation* film, as well as other Aitken films made by Majestic, Reliance and Triangle. Other movie producers also donated prints of their important films. This assures the Museum of Modern Art a permanent collection of early day movies available for showing and study by movie fans, critics, and scholars.

In 1946, our old associate Thomas Dixon died. He was buried in his native North Carolina by friends. A newspaper editor wrote a stirring booklet relating the accomplishments of the fiery orator, preacher, and author.

Then in 1948, disillusioned and broken-hearted, David Griffith died in California. The day we received the news, Harry and I comforted each other. Certainly we had had our differences with Griffith, but one does not forget the bonds that tie people close in times of cooperative endeavor and struggle. Griffith and the Aitkens had shared many dreams and many disappointments. We could not forget that.

Tom Ince had died tragically a number of years earlier. Now, only Sennett, Harry and I remained of the group who once associated in Majestic, Reliance, Keystone, and Triangle productions.

The years slipped by. Then in 1954 Harry received that fateful telephone call from Phil Ryan in Hollywood.

"This could be it," Harry said happily. "I've always felt some producer would want to try a remake of the *Birth*."

When Ryan's negotiations for financing failed, the let-down for Harry and me was agonizing. But it did not take Harry long to bounce back. Though in his seventies, he still had spring in his step and the eagerness of battle in his eyes.

"We've got to continue to promote the *Birth* film more actively," he told me. "If the film continues to show now and then in public theaters, and also in art and university theaters, it will remain in the public eye until the remake comes. We also want to be in trim to take advantage of the opportunity for the remake when it comes."

Harry was in trim up to the moment he died in 1956. He was working actively with a Chicago theater manager who planned to schedule a showing of the *Birth*. During the discussion about the picture in the manager's office, Harry collapsed from a heart attack and died shortly after.

Thus ended the stirring and significant career of one of the men who founded the American motion picture industry and who helped to shape it in its early years—a man who aided many directors and movie players on their way to national recognition.

Mack Sennett, the other of our early day partners, died in 1960.

That leaves me—Roy Aitken—as sole survivor of the Aitken, Griffith, Dixon, Ince, and Sennett organization that had meant so much to all of us. With Harry's death, I inherited his stock and controlling interest in the *Birth of a Nation*. Officially, I am now its sole nursemaid, and what a precocious baby it has been for all these years.

I am busy now and then sending prints of the *Birth* and our other silent pictures to theaters that wish to rent them. I have even had requests for films from England, Denmark, and Canada.

The movie fever which first infected me in 1905 is still racing in my blood. I love to think of those exciting days when Griffith, Dixon, Ince, Sennett, Harry, and I were at the top of filmdom's rushing tide.

In 1959, I was approached by another Hollywood syndicate that wanted to buy my rights in the *Birth of a Nation*. The spokesman said his sponsors wanted to make the *Birth* into a new, salable picture. We couldn't make a deal, however, because the syndicate wanted my *Birth* rights for a song, and I wouldn't sell.

If I live long enough, I may get another Hollywood offer which I could accept. Then Harry's prediction of an effective remake of the *Birth of a Nation* by an established producer may still come true. Whatever happens, I am glad I had the opportunity to take a part in those wonderful, fantastic days of the early "flickers"—days that will never come again, except on a museum screen.

The END